INSIDE THE
BOARDROOM

INSIDE THE BOARDROOM

Governance by Directors and Trustees

William G. Bowen

John Wiley & Sons, Inc.

New York • Chichester • Brisbane • Toronto • Singapore

This text is printed on acid-free paper.

Copyright © 1994 by John Wiley & Sons, Inc.

All rights reserved. Published simultaneously in Canada.

Reproduction or translation of any part of this work beyond
that permitted by Section 107 or 108 of the 1976 United
States Copyright Act without the permission of the copyright
owner is unlawful. Requests for permission or further
information should be addressed to the Permissions Department,
John Wiley & Sons, Inc.

This publication is designed to provide accurate and authoritative
information in regard to the subject matter covered. It is sold
with the understanding that the publisher is not engaged in
rendering legal, accounting, or other professional services. If
legal advice or other expert assistance is required, the services
of a competent professional person should be sought. FROM A
DECLARATION OF PRINCIPLES JOINTLY ADOPTED BY A
COMMITTEE OF THE AMERICAN BAR ASSOCIATION AND
A COMMITTEE OF PUBLISHERS.

Library of Congress Cataloging-in-Publication Data:

Bowen, William G.
    Inside the boardroom : governance by directors and trustees /
William G. Bowen.
        p.   cm.
    Includes index.
    ISBN 0-471-02501-1 (cloth : acid-free paper)
    1. Corporate governance—United States.   2. Directors of
corporations—United States.   3. Trusts and trustees—United States.
I. Title.
HD2785.B68   1994   93-42717
658.4'22—dc20

Printed in the United States of America

10 9 8 7 6

To the Memory of

R. Manning Brown, Jr. and John E. F. Wood
Superb Directors/Trustees and Warm Friends

Contents

Preface

Governance is a fascinating subject. At bottom, it has to do with power and accountability—who exercises power, on behalf of whom, and how the exercise of power is controlled.[1] It involves complex webs of personal as well as institutional relationships. It provides the voyeur with insights into human frailties and strengths at the same time that it provides the student of abstract organizational structures with conundrums. Governance also at least *seems* to be a relatively accessible subject, which may be another reason for its popularity. As one highly experienced board member, John C. Whitehead (now chairman of AEA Investors and formerly co-managing partner of Goldman Sachs and Deputy Secretary of State), puts it: "When it comes to governance, everyone is an expert."

The full effects of "good" versus "bad" governance can be hard to calibrate and are actively debated, but no one doubts that they are real. When things go wrong at major corporations such as General Motors and IBM, there are serious consequences for society at large as well as for the workers, investors, and communities affected most directly. The directors are accountable; it is up to them to guide a reassessment of strategic directions and, if need be, to replace the CEO or see that other managerial changes are made. In the nonprofit sector, too, the media are increasingly critical of boards that seem to be "snoring" while performance deteriorates, as the *New York Times* characterized the situation at Empire Blue Cross.[2] Governing mechanisms are, after all, the steering devices for complex organizations—with the potential to guide them down right or wrong paths.

Any reader of the daily press will be aware that interest in corporate governance has increased dramatically in this country in recent years, in part as a result of increased shareholder activism. Similar efforts to hold boards accountable are now beginning to be seen in other countries. In Switzerland, Japan, Germany, and the United Kingdom, institutional shareholders have demanded that boards pay attention to them, open themselves up to ideas from outside, and even change their structures and habitual forms of operating.[3]

While a variety of reasons may be advanced to explain this globalization of interest in governance, there is no denying the spread of curiosity about how organizations are governed, and how they *should* be governed. "Curiosity" is a right word in that governance is seen by many as a kind of black box that is hard for outsiders to penetrate. And even some of those most intimately involved with for-profit and nonprofit organizations have only a dim sense of where power resides, how it is distributed and exercised, and how it is limited and controlled. One theme of this book is that broader awareness of forms of governance, traditional practices, contentious issues, and new options is highly desirable. All of us, after all, have a stake in how well the organizations in our society are led.

Inside the Boardroom addresses only one aspect of this large subject: the effectiveness—or sometimes the ineffectiveness—of governing boards. If its range is narrow in this respect, it is broad in another: Close attention is paid to both for-profit and nonprofit boards. More specifically, I am referring to boards of "directors" and boards of "trustees," though I often use directors as a generic descriptor for board members in both sectors.

I have been asked what prompted my (by now rather intense) interest in how boards function, and how they should function. It is not, in fact, a new interest. In the nonprofit context, it dates back to the late 1960s, when I was much involved in attempting to think through the governance of universities during the campus controversies that occurred in the aftermath of Vietnam. My interest in corporate governance was first sparked by the takeover movement, the rise of the institutional investor, and the appearance in the business world of the Watergate style of investigative reporting.

More recently, my interest in the governance of for-profit companies has been intensified by personal experiences. I have been a direct participant in some highly charged events (including the takeover of NCR by AT&T and the election of a new CEO at American Express) that have caused me to question whether inherited structures and conventions remain appropriate. Anne Armstrong, a director of General Motors and a colleague of mine on the American Express Board and (until recently) on the Board of Regents of the Smithsonian, observed that it was her participation in several "revolutions" that had caused her to reflect on the topic of governance. It was not prior reflections on governance that had caused her to join the revolutions—though, she suggested, that might have been the preferable order. My own sequencing of experience and thought is the same as Mrs. Armstrong's.

My work at The Andrew W. Mellon Foundation over the past five years has made me much more aware than I was before of the daunting challenges facing boards in many parts of the nonprofit world. Problems arise regularly because of ineffective governance, and it is distressing to see opportunities missed and resources wasted. Growing concern about corporate governance has been mirrored by increasing interest in governance within the nonprofit world—in part because of scarcity of resources, which often provokes (properly) searches for improved ways of operating and sometimes even interest in new ways of managing institutions. In addition, as the experiences of United Way and Empire Blue Cross illustrate (see Appendix B), nonprofit institutions today are subject to more scrutiny by external critics than was once the case.

My own mix of experiences in the for-profit and nonprofit sectors has led to one of the two distinguishing characteristics of this study: its comparative approach. I am convinced that much can be learned by contrasting presumptions and practices in the nonprofit and for-profit arenas. Each has lessons to teach the other, and there is more than a little room for improved performance all around. Contrary to general impressions, nonprofit boards seem to me better positioned than many of their corporate cousins to deal with some recurring problems faced by all boards, including the achievement of the right relationship between the board and the CEO. Nonprofit boards, in turn, have much to learn from disciplines characteristic of corporate boards—especially the routine use of benchmark data and the constant monitoring of discrepancies between results and planned outcomes.

While this comparative orientation is not the usual approach (most of the literature concentrates, sometimes exclusively, on either corporate or nonprofit boards),[4] I believe that some of the most vexing questions are seen in a new light when a conscious effort is made to understand why different models predominate in one sector or the other. An apt analogy for me is foreign travel. When I visited the People's Republic of China in 1974 (shortly after the Cultural Revolution), I came back not only with a new awareness of the problems and opportunities facing that vast country, with a history and a culture so different from our own, but also with a heightened sense of what was special about the United States and its institutions. Characteristics of this society that we take for granted, such as the freedom—and willingness—to express critical opinions in almost any setting, took on a new meaning for me.

This is an avowedly impressionistic study. I have not tried to repress a personal tone.* Nor have I resisted presenting normative propositions. On the contrary, the core of the book consists of a set of 20 "presumptive norms" that I believe should govern how boards function unless there are compelling reasons, in a particular situation, for doing something else. (A colleague of mine, Harriet Zuckerman, describes norms in terms of "the four ps: *p*rescriptions, *p*roscriptions, *p*references, and *p*ermissions." I use the term in her sense, not to indicate what is "normal" or "average.") Appendix A lists these 20 norms. A recurring question is which principles and propositions have some claim on universality and which are highly specific to particular sectors or even to particular organizations in a given sector at a point in time. The search for both similarities and abiding differences runs through the pages that follow.

I make no claim to having made a full scholarly review of a considerable, rapidly growing, body of literature. Nor have I conducted new empirical research. The raw material underlying the text consists primarily of (1) lessons learned while serving on a reasonably wide variety of both corporate and nonprofit boards and (2) extensive conversations and exchanges of correspondence with others who have served in similar capacities.

Personal experiences (especially when they are gripping) can help one see simple points with a new clarity, but they can also lead to erroneous generalizations—which is one reason I have been helped so

---

*One other matter of style should be mentioned. I have found no new solution to the "pronoun problem" and have chosen to use "he" throughout when I want to refer, generically, to an individual of either sex who might be the CEO or the chairman of an organization. (I also prefer not to use "chair" or "chairperson.") The reality is that the corporate world still contains few women in these positions. There are more women in senior positions in the nonprofit world, although there is much room for further progress there, too.

much by criticisms and suggestions offered in response to earlier drafts of this manuscript. In working and reworking this material, and in reviewing and discussing the comments of others, I have become more and more aware of how autobiographical many of us are when we discuss governance. What has worked, or failed to work, for each of us takes on a special aura.

In any case, and in the spirit of full disclosure, the reader should know the associations that have provoked many of the comments that follow—and, by inference, the kinds of experiences I have *not* had, since I am as conscious of the deficiencies of my "preparation" as I am of the unusually rich array of opportunities I have had to learn at first hand about governance. At one time or another, I have served as an outside director of five corporations: American Express, Merck, NCR (until its acquisition by AT&T), Reader's Digest, and Rockefeller Group (which owns Rockefeller Center). I have also served as an outside director of six nonprofit entities: the Center for Advanced Study in the Behavioral Sciences, Denison University, the Public Broadcast Laboratory of National Educational Television, the Sloan Foundation, the Smithsonian Institution, and the Wallace-Reader's Digest Funds. As CEO, I have served on the boards of two other nonprofit institutions: Princeton University and The Andrew W. Mellon Foundation. In addition, and in part as a consequence of the Mellon Foundation's larger interest in the health of the nonprofit sector, I have followed the experiences of organizations (some thriving and some in trouble), in fields ranging from higher education, to ecology, to culture and the performing arts, including organizations as diverse as the American Antiquarian Society, the New York Botanical Gardens, the Population Council, the New-York Historical Society, and Wilson College (in Pennsylvania).

As already noted, I have benefited enormously from a special resource: the observations of numerous colleagues and friends who took the time to comment, often at length, on many of the points made here. Some of their comments were so perceptive, and so well stated, that I have incorporated them directly into the text, with or without attribution as seemed appropriate. One person privy to this correspondence was so impressed by it that he urged me simply to publish the comments "as is." While that was not feasible, I tried to do the next best thing.

The wide range of perspectives and perceptions registered by these commentators led me to modify, and in some instances to change altogether, previous conclusions based on my starting impressions. What started out as "personal impressions" evolved into an unusual kind of collaborative work, with layers of commentary, and occasionally comments on the commentary, interspersed through the text. In this regard, if in no other, the final product may have a kind of Talmudic aspect.

The active involvement of so many sharp-eyed and sharp-tongued commentators, and the interactive character of much of the text, has become the second distinguishing characteristic of this book. Because of the importance I attach to the contributions of the commentators, I list them here, with some of their principal affiliations.

Commentators

Anne L. Armstrong, chairman of the Board of Trustees of the Center for Strategic and International Studies; former Ambassador to the Court of St. James

H. Brewster Atwater, Jr., chairman and CEO of General Mills

Robert L. Banse, former senior vice-president and general counsel of Merck & Co.

Lewis W. Bernard, chairman of Classroom, Inc.; advisory director of Morgan Stanley

Henry S. Bienen, dean of the Woodrow Wilson School of Public and International Affairs, Princeton University

John H. Biggs, chairman and CEO of TIAA/CREF

W. Michael Blumenthal, ltd. partner, Lazard Frères & Co.; former chairman and CEO of UNISYS; former Secretary of the Treasury

Frederick Borsch, Bishop of the Episcopal Diocese of Los Angeles

Jeffrey K. Brinck, partner, Milbank, Tweed, Hadley and McCloy

McGeorge Bundy, scholar in residence, Carnegie Corporation of New York; former president of the Ford Foundation and National Security Advisor

David M. Culver, chairman of CAI Capital Corporation; former chairman and CEO of ALCAM, Aluminium Ltd.

D. Ronald Daniel, treasurer of Harvard University; former managing director of McKinsey & Co.

Ralph D. DeNunzio, former chairman and CEO of Kidder, Peabody Group Inc.

Charles W. Duncan, Jr., investor; former Secretary of U.S. Department of Energy

Charles E. Exley, Jr., former chairman and CEO of NCR

Richard B. Fisher, chairman of Morgan Stanley Group Inc.

Richard M. Furlaud, former chairman and CEO of Squibb Corporation

Ellen Futter, president of the American Museum of Natural History; former president of Barnard College

Louis V. Gerstner, Jr., chairman and CEO of IBM; former chairman and CEO of RJR Nabisco

Robert F. Goheen, president emeritus of Princeton University

William T. Golden, corporate director, trustee

Harvey Golub, chairman and CEO of American Express

Hanna Gray, president emeritus of the University of Chicago

George V. Grune, chairman and CEO of Reader's Digest Association, Inc.

John M. Harris, president and CEO of Rockefeller Financial Services, Inc.

Robert Kasdin, treasurer and chief investment officer of the Metropolitan Museum of Art

Nicholas deB. Katzenbach, counsel, Riker, Danzig, Scherer, Hyland and Perretti; former senior vice-president and general counsel of IBM Corporation; former U.S. Attorney General

Frederick J. Kelly, former dean of the School of Business of Seton Hall University

Organization of the Book

- Chapter 1 introduces the general subject by asking: Why do we have boards? Do they really matter? How much? In what contexts in particular? To what extent do external checks and constraints pre-ordain outcomes, regardless of what boards do or don't do? Are these external checks more significant in for-profit than in nonprofit settings?
- Chapter 2 discusses the functions of boards. To what extent do for-profit and nonprofit boards serve the same functions?

Different functions? What are the most important and most distinctive tasks of boards in the two sectors? How does the distinction between board and staff functions vary across organizations?

- Chapter 3 introduces the idea of "presumptive norms" in the context of how boards are constituted. Is there an optimal size, and are there reasons to expect it to differ between for-profit and nonprofit boards? What can be said about membership and composition, including the relative numbers of inside versus outside directors, key attributes of individual members, diversity of backgrounds and perspectives, independence (including subtle issues of conflict and of excessively close relationships with the CEO), and the wisdom of keeping retired CEOs on a board? Should there be limits on terms of service and a principle of rotation? Should members of nonprofit boards be compensated?

- Chapter 4 is concerned with how boards are organized. It discusses the hotly debated issue of whether the CEO should also chair the board or whether there should be a separate chairman. Are there alternative approaches that will achieve some of the same goals as the election of a separate chairman? What accounts for the radical differences in practice between for-profit and nonprofit organizations in this regard? This chapter also proposes norms for committee structures and the composition of key committees, the use of executive sessions, the direct access of outside board members to expert advisors, and the role of a retiring CEO in the selection of a new CEO.

- Chapter 5 explores how boards are informed. It includes a discussion of differences between the sectors in the provision of data and other information that often determine the capacity of a board to act in a timely way, if at all. Consideration is also given to the effects of accounting conventions (especially fund accounting) on the adequacy of information available to nonprofits. The use of benchmarks and "key indicators" is proposed.

- Chapter 6 is a kind of epilogue, more speculative in tone than earlier chapters. The focus is on the performance on nonprofit boards of individuals with business backgrounds—and on the reasons their performance often seems disappointing.

- There is a brief conclusion consisting mainly of a summary of principal themes.

- There are also two appendixes. Appendix A lists all 20 of the presumptive norms discussed in the book. Appendix B provides capsule profiles of four for-profit and five nonprofit organizations cited with some frequency in the text.

Acknowledgments

In addition to the commentators listed earlier, I want to thank the remarkable group of colleagues and friends who have done so much to encourage me along the way. At the Mellon Foundation, I have enjoyed the steadfast support of the trustees, including the chairman of the board, John C. Whitehead. In addition to Mr. Whitehead, Charles Exley, Hanna Gray, and Frank Rhodes are listed among the commentators, and all members of the board have understood and supported my interest in studying and writing about problems related to the Foundation's grant-making activities.

Among my colleagues on the staff of the Foundation, I want to express special thanks to:

- Joan Gilbert, research coordinator in our Princeton office, who has taken primary responsibility for helping me with all facets of this book, and for shepherding it through its final stages.

- T. Dennis Sullivan, financial vice-president, who has been a never-ending source of encouragement and sharp insight from the time we first discussed the subject of governance by boards.

- Harriet Zuckerman, vice-president, who has a deep understanding of the principles of governance and who is also a superb editor.
- Kamla Motihar, the Foundation's librarian, who constantly amazes all of us by her ability to find anything and everything instantly.
- Sarah E. Turner, now a doctoral candidate in economics at the University of Michigan, who has contributed both an analytical perspective to the framing of the study and many suggestions concerning content and tone.
- Other members of the research staff—Jed Bergman, Kevin Guthrie, and especially Tom Nygren—who have taken time from their own projects to help with this one.
- Members of the program staff and senior advisors—Rachel Bellow, Stephanie Bell-Rose, Henry Drewry, Richard Ekman, Alice Emerson, Alvin Kernan, Carolyn Makinson, Richard E. Quandt, William Robertson, Eileen Scott, and Kellum Smith—who have sharpened my understanding of what transpires in substantive areas in which each is expert.
- Other colleagues on the support staff, including Ulrica Konvalin, Margaret McKenna, Martha Sullivan, and Dorothy Westgate, who have done whatever was asked of them—and volunteered to do more.

I also want to thank my friends at John Wiley & Sons, including Charles Ellis (who provided early encouragement), Ruth Mills, and Karl Weber, for their help in transforming an idea into a book. They have been very patient with me.

WILLIAM G. BOWEN

1

The Importance of Boards

It is helpful to ask, right at the start: Why do we have boards of directors and boards of trustees at all? Why has this mechanism seemed preferable in so many instances to other modes of governance? The existence of boards is tied to the corporate form of organizational structure, as distinguished from the partnership or the unincorporated enterprise such as a family business, and the legal advantages of the corporate form (with limited liability and other protections for individuals) are well known. Nonprofits, as well as for-profits, benefit from them. In addition, it is almost always easiest for nonprofits to satisfy regulatory requirements by incorporating and operating with the usual kind of governing board.

There is, however, also a deeper set of considerations that I hope will emerge in the following pages. Both for-profit and nonprofit entities operate in inherently complex settings, where matters are rarely cut and dried. The exercise of collective responsibility through a board can slow down some kinds of decision making, but it can also dampen the enthusiasm of the aspiring autocrat. It provides checks and balances by adding layers of judgment and protections against abuse of power and some forms of self-dealing, self-promoting, and favoritism. The existence of a board also encourages the development of an institutional sense of purpose and continuity.

Granted these advantages, boards are far from perfect instruments, and the main purpose of this book is to suggest ways in which they can function better. For most complex entities, however, I remain convinced that the idea of a board of directors or trustees, when translated into effective decision-making mechanisms and invested with well-chosen members, is preferable as a principle of organization to any known alternative.

Positive and Negative Effects of Board Governance

My short answer, then, to the question of whether boards matter is that they *can* and *should* matter a great deal, and not only when a crisis is at hand. In fact, I would argue that they are potentially most important well "before the storm," when thoughtful board members can help to identify impending problems and encourage the adoption of measures that will prevent a possible crisis from ever developing. Boards can also matter greatly as negative forces when they either act imprudently or fail to anticipate major changes in, for example, technology, marketplaces, or (for nonprofits) contributions from public or private donors.

We can all think of examples of both foresight and lack of foresight—many attributable to CEOs and presidents, to be sure, but some assignable in no small part to boards themselves, and especially to key directors or trustees. Let me first cite two examples of foresight—one with which I am personally familiar from the nonprofit world and another from the for-profit sector.

In the years immediately after World War II, the investment committee of the Princeton Board was led by a trustee named Dean Mathey (he was a sophisticated New York investor, most assuredly not an academic dean). Mr. Mathey persuaded his colleagues to invest a significant portion of the university's endowment in common stocks—and even in start-up ventures such as McDonald's—at a time when much of the conventional wisdom regarded bonds as the only prudent investment for a college or university.

That one decision had an enormous impact. More than any other single factor, it was responsible for the relatively large size of the Princeton endowment today. Dean Mathey convinced his fellow trustees to make a strategic decision that must have seemed to many of them to be—at best—ahead of its time. A staunch conservative, Mathey took great satisfaction in telling those who thought he was deserting his principles: "The only true test of conservatism is to be right in the future."

Among for-profit corporations on whose boards I have served, the history of NCR, back in the (for NCR) preelectronic era, is particularly relevant. The directors of the company at that time were wise enough to recognize that old ways could not be sustained. The era of the mechanical cash register and accounting machine was at an end, and the fortunes of the company were declining rapidly; absent strong action, it might have failed altogether. The directors decided to recruit a new CEO and had the perspicacity to choose a relatively unknown executive in Japan, Bill Anderson, who did nothing less than move the company into the modern world, finding an appropriate niche for it in the computer industry.

It is all too easy to refer to recent examples of disappointing performances by boards of directors in both the for-profit and nonprofit sectors. Much has been written about the slowness of the board of General Motors to adopt strategies that would work in a much more competitive world market for motor vehicles—a market which treated harshly a high-cost producer that seemed out of touch with the preferences of many buyers. Similar observations have been made about the evident need at American Express to address the profound changes occurring in the credit card business.[1] Most recently, the directors of Paramount were criticized for not acting with sufficient independence from the CEO-chairman, Martin Davis, in evaluating bids for the company.[2]

A widely publicized failure of a nonprofit board to act properly was the prolonged neglect of its extraordinary collection of Native American art by the trustees of the Heye Foundation. The Attorney General of New York eventually intervened and the board was almost entirely reconstituted; but by then the difficulties of caring for the collection, and exhibiting it properly, had become overwhelming. Arrangements were made to transfer responsibility for the collection to the Smithsonian Institution in Washington, D.C.[3]

Mentioning these few cases illustrates not only the wide range of problems that boards must confront but also the marked differences in settings. Each organization operates in its own environment and faces its own constituencies and constraints. The ease with which it is possible to document positive and negative contributions by boards (with failures almost always easier to identify than successes) should not delude us into thinking that directors can "do anything." Boards sometimes operate within very confining contexts, and it would be a mistake to minimize the importance of less visible but powerful economic, political, and social forces—to succumb to a kind of "great board" theory of corporate history.

Indeed, the functioning of boards can be understood only if we first recognize the forces that circumscribe their behavior. While all boards need to have a sophisticated sense of what their own environments will allow them to do, a principal theme of this chapter is that the nature and extent of external constraints vary markedly between the for-profit and nonprofit sectors. In general, for-profit boards face tighter constraints, largely because of the role played by market forces.

How the Market Regulates For-Profit Corporations

The best known for-profit companies operate in public markets, and dissatisfied shareholders can register displeasure simply by disposing of their stock. Companies are subject to Securities and Exchange Commission (SEC) disclosure requirements, and information on profits, sales, and industry trends is widely available. Share prices are quoted constantly, and movements in market valuations represent more or less instantaneous votes of confidence (or of no confidence) in corporate actions or inactions.

Moreover, large-scale transactions, perhaps involving the purchase or sale of a subsidiary and sometimes even an entire entity, can occur quite suddenly in response to changed circumstances or new opportunities. Thus, for-profit organizations may have their futures altered dramatically by external buyers or sellers, as anyone who has participated in a corporate merger or takeover, friendly or unfriendly, will attest. In such situations, the ultimate sanction is a proxy vote by shareholders to unseat recalcitrant directors. Having been unseated myself (in company with the other members of my "class" of directors, in the final stages of the AT&T takeover of NCR), I can attest to the reality of this final source of shareholder power!

More generally and less dramatically, capital markets are constantly regulating the behavior of most for-profit companies, especially those that cannot rely solely on retained earnings to finance themselves. In many situations, corporate strategies and their implementation are applauded or dismissed through third-party decisions to provide or withhold capital. Investors, financial institutions, and the markets themselves are meant to ration capital, and they do, usually in an efficient way. Specialists in industrial organization and corporate finance will continue to debate just how efficient capital markets really are, whether or not "short-termism" is a serious malady in the United States today, and if complaints of "underinvestment" in certain fields are justified.[4] Similarly, there are differences of opinion as to whether the decline in hostile takeovers has removed an important source of pressure on managements and boards.[5] No one doubts, however, that markets in general (including markets for products, ideas, and personnel, as well as for capital) influence and ultimately constrain board decisions.

But this is hardly to say that the existence of markets makes governance by boards irrelevant. Much room remains for decision making. We are not living in an "Adam Smith age" in which atomistic units respond automatically to the signals provided by impersonal market forces. There are plenty of opportunities for boards to make big mistakes, just as there are opportunities to find the right new direction before others do. Management and governance plainly matter.

In recent years, the role of the institutional investor in influencing boards has been discussed at length. There is no denying that institutional investors have been in the forefront of broad-based efforts to influence and improve corporate governance—and in this role have been, and can be, quite effective. Some believe that political pressures generated by large shareholders will come to have even more far-reaching effects, replacing takeovers, and threats of takeovers, as the dominant external constraint on companies in the 1990s.[6]

Others argue that increasing activism on the part of institutional investors is unlikely to substitute in any significant degree for effective governance by boards as traditionally constituted. As Lipton and Lorsch explain cogently, institutional investors find it difficult to act like the large individual owners of the past: They hold shares in too many companies, often use indexing, and are subject to various legal and other constraints. Their conclusion is that *direct* participation in governance by large institutional investors is, in the main, unlikely—and probably a bad idea anyway.[7]

The problems encountered by some of the so-called relationship investors* in attracting funds illustrate the limits on the role that institutional investors are likely to play in making substantive decisions—at least in the case of large companies. (In small, privately

---

*Defined as investors who take large positions in the stock of companies and occupy board seats to influence the directions taken by management and to monitor their "relationship" with the companies.

held companies, major investors routinely sit on the board, have direct influence on strategic decisions, and sometimes even make operating decisions.) All of us may want to believe that "patient money" will be rewarded, if it is invested in a company with prospects as well as problems, and if it is combined with the presence on the board of one or more highly competent outside directors representing the patient investor. Still, there appears to be some skepticism, especially among the large institutional investors who might be expected to support this approach, concerning the probability of earning above-average returns by pursuing such a strategy.[8] It may be that the risk of betting on improved governance to achieve superior results is too great for at least certain classes of investors.

A number of empirical studies have correlated indexes of corporate structure and governance with measures of economic and financial outcomes. This is not easy research, and the results are often far from clear-cut. A recent survey of the literature supports the view that board oversight and monitoring by institutional investors improves corporate performance, though the evidence cannot be regarded as overwhelming.[9] We are left then, with the usual mixed verdict: governance matters, but so do a host of other factors. Governance, like scholarship, should be taken seriously, but it should also be kept "in its place."[10]

Its place may be rather different, however, in the for-profit and nonprofit sectors. I have come to believe that boards often have considerably greater influence, for better or for worse, in the nonprofit sector than in the for-profit world.

Degrees of Freedom and Accountability for Nonprofits

Nonprofits face numerous constraints of their own, which differ in both kind and intensity from one subfield to another (contrast, for example, the circumstances of regulated day-care centers and independent libraries such as the Frick Collection). Important as they are, however, these constraints tend to be less circumscribing than those encountered by directors of for-profit entities. External, market-driven forces play a *relatively* weaker role in determining outcomes in the nonprofit sector. There is, if you will, more room for institutionally driven factors to influence outcomes, and this is the principal reason I am persuaded that effective governance is potentially more important in this sector than it is in the for-profit sector.

One commentator (Robert Banse, retired general counsel of Merck) objected to this assertion on the grounds that the ultimate social consequences of good or bad performance are so much greater in the for-profit sector than in the nonprofit sector. If companies such as GM and IBM head in wrong directions, many jobs are lost, real income declines, and so on. Thus, it is argued, even if governance has a more modest impact in the for-profit sector, it may end up making more difference to the world at large. This is not a debate I wish to pursue since my focus is on the effects of governance on *individual institutions,* each of which is presumed to be important in its own way. But there is wisdom in remembering the commonsense point that not all organizations, in either sector, are of equal importance. We should also note that the nonprofit sector itself contains a number of very large institutions and has become highly consequential overall. It contains over one million entities, originates about 6 percent of the gross national product, and employs roughly 10 percent of all workers in the United States.[11]

I certainly do not want to suggest that any nonprofit entity is free of constraints (often tough ones), imposed by the realities of what are, in effect, its own "markets." These markets contain pools of potential volunteers, donors, and purchasers of services; and nonprofit entities of every stripe compete vigorously and sometimes even voraciously for their allegiance. Performing arts organizations need to sell tickets, service providers must find clients, colleges must enroll students, and nonprofit entities of all kinds have to recruit volunteers and, year after year, persuade potential donors of their virtues. Life in many parts of the nonprofit world is demanding and difficult for those with oversight responsibilities—often more demanding and difficult, for the managements at least, than life in parts of the for-profit world, conventional images and assumptions notwithstanding.

Nonetheless, managements and boards of most nonprofits retain more degrees of freedom than do their counterparts in the for-profit world. This is true, first, because nonprofits can choose among a wider variety of objectives, and can assign a wider variety of weights to different objectives, than can for-profit entities, which are presumed by their shareholders and others to have earnings and profits always in mind.* In the nonprofit world, outputs and outcomes are harder to measure, and constituencies are harder to define. There is no single measure of success, or even of progress, that is analogous to the proverbial bottom line for a business.

The significance of multiple objectives can be illustrated by citing an example from the field of higher education. In seeking to understand shifts in the arts-and-sciences share of BA degrees conferred by educational institutions in the 1960s, my colleague

---

*In fact, however, objectives are also more complex in the for-profit sector than is sometimes thought. Without entering into the continuing debate over "stakeholder" versus "shareholder" claims on a company, let me simply assert that most companies today (certainly all large, highly visible companies) must be attuned to the concerns and needs of their employees, customers, vendors, and the communities in which they operate—in part because this makes good business sense and in part because companies are part of the nation's social fabric and cannot escape the attendant responsibilities. Even in pursuing purely financial objectives, companies can choose among many measures of value, from current income to growth in earnings per share to return on assets or on shareholders' equity. Also, as discussed in Chapter 5, companies are paying more and more attention to nonfinancial measures of performance. It is easy to exaggerate the significance of apparently simple measures of success such as earnings per share, looked at on their own.

Sara Turner and I surmised that one important group of colleges and universities chose to "spend" increased student demand for places at their institutions on efforts to enhance their academic standing. They did so by increasing their offerings in the arts and sciences, and they apparently gave greater weight to this objective than to increasing enrollment in more vocationally oriented fields, thereby presumably forgoing the opportunity to earn higher net revenues, at least in the short run. For-profit educational institutions would almost surely have responded quite differently to the enrollment boom of the 1960s.[12]

Nonprofit boards enjoy more freedom of action than their for-profit cousins for another reason. As a general rule, fundamental choices can be made by nonprofit institutions without anyone worrying that these decisions may be subject to abrupt reversal by market forces—or, for that matter, by outside forces of any kind. After all, nonprofit entities are not routinely for sale, and mergers and closings tend to occur only when nonprofit institutions are in deep trouble. In many situations, there is no body of watchful critics. Moreover, there are few publicly available indicators for critics to watch even if there were observers inclined to look for them.

Consequences of Unexamined Lives

A worrying corollary is that at least some nonprofits may lead lives that are simultaneously undistinguished and largely unnoticed. Organizations may be allowed to function in a basically unsatisfactory way for years without many people being aware of the situation and without anyone blowing a loud whistle. To be sure, the degree of public scrutiny varies greatly within the nonprofit sector. Hospitals and other health-care providers are under closer and closer surveillance. Colleges and universities are also closely scrutinized, since they must deal with students (and student reporters!), alumni, faculty (the most demanding group of all), parents, government auditors and agencies, legislators, donors and, increasingly, the media and outside commentators. Recall the public pillorying of Stanford University for its handling of indirect costs.

The "glass bowl" character of governance in such settings assures one kind of accountability and can be a protection against serious blunders. But it is also true, as several friends have pointed out, that such scrutiny can consist almost exclusively of efforts to represent group interests and to marshall opposition to needed changes. As one person put it, "Outcries result from attempts to improve performance by interfering with time-honored conventions or tampering with special interests." The conservative tendencies of faculty, alumni, and other groups can inhibit risk taking and, for that matter, any change whatsoever. Intense external scrutiny can also focus attention on the wrong issues, thereby diverting energies from questions that are more fundamental, if less interesting to the world at large. On balance, however, the relatively high degree of scrutiny characteristic of institutions of higher education seems to me beneficial. I know far less about the health-care field, but I suspect that the same conclusion holds there.

There is, as always, an opposite end to the spectrum. The part of the nonprofit sector in which I now work, the world of the large private foundations, is perhaps most insulated of all from external checks. In addition, there are not many truly objective measures of success or failure, which makes it still harder even for insiders to know if the foundation is doing as well as it should do. Also, there are few other constituencies that can challenge the leadership. In contrast to the university world, there are no faculty members, students, parents, or grantors to function as counterweights, and grantees are usually reluctant—too reluctant, I believe—to criticize or to complain.

As a result, a great deal depends on the quality of the staff and the oversight exercised by trustees. In my view, the trustees of foundations have more opportunity to affect institutional performance than do the directors of any other set of entities in either the for-profit or nonprofit sector. Such opportunities obviously can be used wisely, wasted, or even abused—which raises the hard question of how to assess the stewardship of these trustees.

Overall, it is fair to say that nonprofits as a group are *far* less closely monitored externally than are for-profit organizations. If a company is at all well known, security analysts will follow it and publish their assessments. Detailed information of various kinds is required by the SEC and other regulatory authorities. Rating agencies collect their own data. All information about the company that can be obtained, by fair means or foul, will be discussed by the business press, which has become much more aggressive. Institutional shareholders will expect to be briefed and will not hesitate to raise questions and criticisms. Annual meetings should offer yet another opportunity for shareholders in general to raise questions and challenge both management and the directors.* Litigation and the attendant process of discovery may unearth a wide range of exotic material. Novels may be written and movies made.

Nonprofits, in sharp contrast, have no well-defined "owners" or external overseers (apart from the board itself), and there are only rather poor substitutes for them. The Internal Revenue Service devotes far less time to scrutinizing the returns of nonprofits than the returns of profit-making entities, for the simple reason that there is so little tax revenue to be claimed. In extremis, the attorney general of the state in which the nonprofit entity operates (or is chartered), or

---

*I say "should" because recent experiences with shareholder participation in annual meetings have increased my own skepticism that this is an effective mechanism. When publicity-seeking "professional activists" such as Evelyn Y. Davies and John Gilbert are allowed to dominate meetings and to create a semi-circus atmosphere, it is hard for ordinary shareholders with serious questions to summon up the courage to go to a microphone. Something has plainly gone wrong, and some combination of courage and new ideas is needed if more annual meetings are to serve as occasions for serious discussion.

the courts in that state, will become involved—but only in extremis. These representatives of the public interest are, ultimately, the owners in the nonprofit world of the underlying assets, but they exercise a far different degree of oversight than do owners and their surrogates in the for-profit world.[13]

External Overseers of Nonprofits

There are, however, some "quasi-owners" in the nonprofit sector who are likely to exert influence well before the attorney general or the courts are aware of a problem. In the case of membership organizations, the "members" themselves serve this function. Individual directors and trustees are a second broad class of potential watchdogs. While the law is not as clear as it might be concerning "standing" in the nonprofit sector (who can bring suit against trustees, directors, or officers in a court), both members and directors plainly have this right.[14] Beyond these groups, however, accountability is hard to fix, short of the attorney general. In the usual case, no constituency has legal power to elect trustees or directors; most nonprofit boards are self-perpetuating.*

While large donors may be thought to constitute another set of quasi-owners, since their largesse is critical to the long-term well-being of many organizations, the law has a quite different view of the situation. Thus, the Annenberg School for Communication at the University of Pennsylvania would not call Walter Annenberg its "owner," even after his recent $125 million gift, and the Internal

---

*Boards of private colleges and universities sometimes choose to allow their alumni (less frequently, faculty or students) to elect some number of trustees, but this is done by choice, not by requirement. Membership organizations such as the NAACP usually have processes for electing members of their boards that are even more participatory. In any case, we should not exaggerate the true differences between for-profits and nonprofits in the selection of directors/trustees. De facto, the boards of most publicly held corporations are also self-perpetuating, short of a major crisis or takeover.

Revenue Service would certainly not accept any such identification. As a matter of law, once a tax-deductible gift has been made, the donor has no continuing claim to power with regard to the use of the funds. We can recall Henry Ford's anguished departure statement, when it became clear the board of the Ford Foundation was going to continue moving in directions other than the ones he favored.[15] Courts have usually denied standing to donors who were displeased with the uses made of their gifts.

Legalities and unusual cases notwithstanding, nonprofits are most reluctant to offend generous patrons. This is partly a matter of feelings of obligation and of good faith—respecting wishes and intentions. Trustees of foundations may well hearken back to the interests of a principal donor when considering to whom they ought to feel responsible. In other contexts, respect for the views of donors can be a matter of prudence—especially if the donors are still alive and might make further gifts. Boards of colleges and universities are often sensitive to the likely response of alumni to decisions they might make, as are boards of all nonprofit organizations with established donor bases.

More generally, "accountability" is usually related to "dependence," and any nonprofit that is dependent on a particular individual, corporation, or constituency will pay more than passing attention to the views of the individual, entity, or group in question, even in the absence of legally enforceable rights. This is why the boards of nonprofits that value their independence attach such importance to diversity of funding sources. Most nonprofits are dependent on far more than donors, and the same principles apply to audiences, clients (including governmental clients in the case of many service-providing nonprofits) and other potential purchasers of services. Nonprofits that lack a well-established base of donors or that must rely on their continued ability to attract substantial earned income can be nearly as likely to go out of business as a family restaurant or small shop. Exit rates in some parts of the nonprofit universe turn out to be appreciably higher than might have been expected, though exits are heavily concentrated among new, and small, entities.*

The wide range of circumstances notwithstanding, significant numbers of nonprofits still function for years, sometimes struggling along, without attracting the attention of powerful outsiders. In many cases, founding donors may be board members themselves, and thus insiders. (This can lead to yet another set of problems, especially if the founding donor has erratic or idiosyncratic views, which other board members are afraid to challenge for fear of upsetting the individual who is paying all, or almost all, the bills.) Dominant donors may be deceased. Or there may be no constituency powerful enough to command attention.

In fact, since they lack most of the mechanisms for radical transformation that markets represent, some nonprofits may well survive too long. The questions of when—and how—to transform or even to dissolve a nonprofit entity are of great significance as issues of public policy, but they attract attention only when some combination of the press and political interests alerts the general public to the travails of an organization such as the New-York Historical Society (see Appendix B). Generally speaking, by the time this kind of alert has been sounded, a number of perhaps promising options will have been closed off altogether or made much more expensive.

---

*Using newly analyzed data from IRS files, Sarah Turner has calculated that the average annual exit rate for all charitable nonprofits in recent years has been just over 2 percent. That is, roughly 2 percent of the organizations active in one year had become "inactive" (according to IRS definitions) the next year. Turner has also found large differences in exit rates by type of organization; for example, the exit rate for performing arts organizations and for organizations concerned with job creation is about three times higher than the exit rate for historical societies. She also finds a definite inverse correlation between exit rates and organizational age and size, confirming again that "the liability of newness" is real. Very few well-established nonprofits cease their activities.

More thought needs to be given, in my view, to ways of allowing nonprofits to achieve "death with dignity" when that is appropriate. In theory, some nonprofits recognize that institutional demise can signal success, not failure. Mission statements of some civil rights groups or advocacy organizations say, in effect, "We hope that, eventually, our service will no longer be needed."* But it can be very hard for an organization with a "sitting" president, staff, and board to dissolve itself. We need to make it easier for organizations, as well as for individuals (and even countries), to declare victory and move on.

My conclusions, then, are that governance does matter, in both for-profit and nonprofit sectors, in good times and bad times, and perhaps especially in those situations in which external checks are minimal and market determinants of outcomes are relatively unimportant. While effective governance is plainly desirable everywhere, it has even more potential to make a difference in the nonprofit sector than in the for-profit sector.

---

*For example, my colleague, Rachel Bellow, has called my attention to the Free Southern Theater in New Orleans, which was founded in the late 1960s in conjunction with the civil rights movement. Its founder decided sometime in the mid-1970s to close the theater, even though it was doing well at the box office, because key objectives had been achieved. The theater staged a large funeral through the streets of New Orleans and artists from all over the country attended to celebrate the "death" (read: success) of the theater.

2

The Functions and Activities of Boards

At the most general level, Lewis Bernard has suggested that all boards share a single overarching responsibility: "to build an effective organization." Everything else is derivative. In the same spirit, Kenneth Dayton has insisted, "Governance is governance."[1] Yet another wise and experienced person, Nicholas Katzenbach, has argued that for-profit and nonprofit boards differ fundamentally in what they are and in what they do.

This is not an argument that can be settled in the abstract (and I can report that commentators are split almost equally between the Dayton and Katzenbach camps). So much depends on the level of abstraction with which a person is comfortable and on whether the emphasis is on *process* or *characteristic activities*. Both approaches have value, as I hope to show in this chapter.

In the interest of clarity, it is important to recognize the varieties of organizations within each of the two broadly defined sectors: "For-profit" and "nonprofit" represent too gross a classification system. At the minimum, we must distinguish for-profit boards that are publicly owned from for-profit boards that are privately held. We must also distinguish charitable nonprofits (which are eligible to receive tax-deductible contributions) from other nonprofits such as labor unions and trade associations; and then, within the charitable group, we must distinguish service providers and grant-seekers from grant-makers (foundations).

Many other distinctions could be introduced. In both the for-profit and nonprofit sectors, and in all subsectors, size, revenue sources, and the degree of family control are significant. Companies in one industry or field are subject to quite different regulatory requirements than are others (for example, banks and other financial institutions fall under the purview of the Glass-Steagall Act, whereas "industrial" corporations do not). Charitable nonprofits differ according to their respective missions, which are critically important in determining all else (museums are very different from civil rights organizations, which in turn differ in fundamental ways from both nursing homes and colleges).

I will not go far down these paths, however, because of the risk of straying too far afield. In what follows, my focus, unless otherwise indicated, is on (1) the large, publicly owned and widely traded for-profit corporations, and (2) the service-providing, grant-seeking nonprofits. I also make occasional comments about the governance of foundations when such information is useful for comparative purposes.

Principal Functions of a Board of Directors or Trustees

At the most basic level, essentially all boards serve six principal functions:

1. *To select, encourage, advise, evaluate and, if need be, replace the CEO.*

Walter Bagehot once described the constitutional authority of the monarch as "the right to be consulted, the right to encourage, the right to warn." In this context, we add the right to elect and the right to dismiss. While "electing" and "dismissing" are actions that need to be taken collectively, "encouraging" and "warning" are often done by individual board members, as well as by the board as a whole.

> 2. *To review and adopt long-term strategic directions and to approve specific objectives, financial and other.*

In the case of both for-profit and nonprofit organizations, this involves taking the long view and protecting against excessive emphasis on short-term considerations. In the case of nonprofit institutions, it also includes reviewing the basic mission of the organization in the light of changed circumstances.

> 3. *To ensure, to the extent possible, that the necessary resources, including human resources, will be available to pursue the strategies and achieve the objectives.*

All boards have a collective responsibility to approve management compensation and to review succession planning. In the case of nonprofits dependent on contributions, individual trustees also need to be responsible advocates, to make meaningful personal financial commitments, and to accept fund-raising responsibility.

> 4. *To monitor the performance of management.*
>
> 5. *To ensure that the organization operates responsibly as well as effectively.*

This includes reviewing the adequacy of policies and procedures for compliance with legal and ethical standards.

6. *To nominate suitable candidates for election to the board, and to establish and carry out an effective system of governance at the board level, including evaluation of board performance.*

What Boards Actually Do

As already noted, the corporate form of organization is common to for-profit and nonprofit entities, and Dayton is right in calling attention to the similarities in the basic responsibilities of directors and trustees. The principal functions I have outlined apply to both. However, while such inventories are useful in organizing our thoughts about the generic functions of boards, they cannot capture behavioral realities. Katzenbach is right in insisting that the characteristic *activities* of boards (what they do, viewed substantively) are quite different in the two sectors—and often quite different within each.

Characteristic Differences between For-Profit and Nonprofit Boards

At the risk of oversimplification, I would suggest that there are three principal differences related to guiding the organization's mission, reviewing its performance, and raising revenue.

Guiding the Organization's Mission

First on my list, and by far the most important, relates to mission:

- *For-profit boards concentrate on developing and carrying out broad strategies for enhancing shareholder values; nonprofit boards are much more committed to the particular "missions" of their own organizations.*

For-profit boards have no obligation whatsoever to pursue any particular line of business, and they may consider, quite consciously, a wide range of strategic directions. Conglomerates illustrate the point most clearly. The objective of the enterprise is not to continue doing any particular thing indefinitely, but rather to find the best way of deploying the company's capital and other resources. Mergers, acquisitions, and divestments are natural activities. No one is surprised to find that U.S. Steel has become USX. Indeed, a key responsibility of for-profit boards is to identify businesses that should be sold off, as well as to probe the desirability of striking out in quite new directions. William Shanklin has remarked that to be faithful to any product line either on the basis of sunk costs or tradition is "to sow the seeds of decline."[2]

The directors of nonprofits, in contrast, have not only the same duties of "care" and "loyalty" as all board members in both sectors,* but also what Daniel Kurtz calls a "duty of obedience."[3] This additional obligation commits these directors to "act with fidelity to the organization's stated mission, within the bounds of the law." If a nonprofit board wishes to alter the fundamental objectives of the organization, "the participation and assent of some representative of the general public—for example, a state attorney general—and the agreement of a court may be required."[4]

Thus, in the nonprofit world, "Organization itself has to be an outgrowth of mission and purpose" (comment by Hanna Gray, president emeritus of the University of Chicago). In her words:

---

*The duty of care concerns a director's competence in performing directorial functions and typically requires directors to use the "care that an ordinarily prudent person would exercise in a like position and under similar circumstances." The "business judgment" rule has been crafted to constrain courts from interfering inappropriately with business decisions made by the management or the board of a for-profit corporation. The duty of loyalty requires the director's faithful pursuit of the interests of the organization rather than the financial or other interests of the director or another person or organization. The concern here is with self-dealing and conflicts of interest.

There are basic reasons why academic institutions are organized and governed as they are, in the service of education and research and of excellence in these pursuits. Faculty are not just "professionals" with a commitment to their professions outside the institution as well as to the institution, or "staff" like museum curators or foundation staff, or odd types who tend to want collegial and complex decision-making. They are individual talents and intellectual entrepreneurs, demanding developers of their disciplines . . . who have in fact certain constitutional rights in the process of governance and who hold the most important authority that exists in a university, that of making ultimate academic judgments. And boards exist in part to ensure this freedom and creativity and to protect the processes and the health of the environment that make them possible. In short, they exist for the sustenance of a mission, for the perpetuation of an institution in which it is embodied over time in such a way that the future is not mortgaged to the present and, by fiduciary obligation, for the direct care and preservation of corporate assets entrusted specifically for the pursuit of a particular mission and its related goals.

This eloquent statement obviously applies specifically to academic institutions; other charitable nonprofits would define themselves in entirely different ways. It is no more likely that a nonprofit dedicated to improving the neighborhood on the south side of Chicago would become a university than it is that the University of Chicago would forget why it was created. Nonprofits are a more variegated lot than are for-profits precisely because each can be expected to have a strong attachment to a particular mission.

In emphasizing this difference in attitudes toward mission between for-profits and nonprofits, I certainly do not mean to suggest that for-profits have no interest in maintaining historic ties to particular fields of activity—it would be hard to think of the Ford Motor Company as uninvolved with automobiles. But the degree and duration of commitment are not the same. Harvard University is the oldest "corporation" on the American continent and has been a leading institution of higher education for more than three centuries. In contrast, the composition of the list of companies in the Fortune 500 has been in constant flux. Of the 500 companies on the list in 1955, only about half (262) were still there in 1980, and many of these had changed significantly, usually as a result of mergers and acquisitions. All told, the companies on the list in 1980 had absorbed nearly 4,500 other companies over the previous 25 years.[5]

Nor do I mean to imply that nonprofits, while concentrating their activities on the pursuit of a defined mission, are precluded from expanding, entering new territories, and so on. Nonprofits may, and often do, extend their reach—wisely or unwisely—for either programmatic or financial reasons. Indeed, the "nondistribution constraint," which prohibits nonprofits from even considering the option of returning any excess funds to "owners," inclines them toward expansion. In recent years, the tendency of some nonprofits to seek more and more ways of increasing earned income has provoked considerable controversy, including debate over the applicability and effectiveness of the tax on unrelated business income. How far to go in these directions is a key question for board members of many nonprofits, since they must respect both the boundaries imposed by a relatively fixed definition of the mission of the institution and the applicable provisions of the law.[6]

Setting aside complications and qualifications, John Whitehead has provided a succinct summary statement of the central point:

> A for-profit board has an obligation to *get out* of a bad business while a nonprofit board may have an obligation to *stay in*, if it is to be true to its mission.

This basic distinction drives much of the content of board deliberations and must be kept in mind in considering all that is said in subsequent chapters about constituting and organizing boards.

Reviewing the Organization's Performance

The second difference in characteristic activities is much more mundane:

- *Corporate boards devote much more time to reviews of performance (short-term and long-term) than do boards of nonprofits.*

This difference in the allocation of time is due in part to the greater ease of measuring at least certain dimensions of performance in the for-profit sector. There is also more of a "bottom-line" mentality in the business world. After all, owners and analysts are watching closely; they look at each quarter's results. In consequence, business boards sometimes spend less time than they should thinking about deeper questions, many of which don't lend themselves to quantification. The boards of nonprofits, on the other hand, are notoriously subject to the problem of failing to see a fast, clearly visible train coming—even when it is moving inexorably and their organization is sitting right on the tracks.

Raising Revenue

The third principal difference in characteristic activities is rooted in different sources of revenue:

- *Many nonprofit boards (though by no means all) must devote a great deal of time and energy to mobilizing volunteers and raising money; also, boards of nonprofits with significant endowments or other monetary assets generally oversee directly the investment of the funds entrusted to the institution.*

These functions are vital to the success of those nonprofits dependent on voluntary contributions, and even to their survival.

Many nonprofit boards work exceptionally hard at managing relationships with important external sources of support, public and private. While staff members, and the president or CEO in particular, have critically important fund-raising roles, there is no substitute for active, effective efforts on the part of key trustees in planning and conducting both special campaigns and ongoing fund-raising activities. This set of board responsibilities includes articulating the rationale for supporting the institution and its programs.

One of my colleagues, Rachel Bellow, has suggested that the need to spend considerable time "away from the table" (including making regular appearances at benefits and other public events) may lead some trustees of nonprofits to feel less responsibility for the standard "at-the-table" tasks of board members. They have, some of them may think, already done their bit for the organization.

For-profit boards are also concerned about the standing of their enterprises with a multiplicity of external constituencies: government regulators, rating agencies, investors, customers, suppliers, and local communities. But management is normally expected to handle these relationships without a great deal of involvement on the part of the board as a whole. (Individual directors with particularly relevant experiences may be asked to help in special situations.)

Trustees of nonprofit entities that are fortunate enough to have sizable endowments typically discharge their responsibilities as investors by recruiting board members with special skills in this area and establishing investment committees. Nonprofit boards are less likely to delegate responsibility for investing their monetary capital to management or staff than are large corporations. The explanation for this difference involves traditional notions of what it means to be a fiduciary (especially of funds that have been entrusted to the trustees by generous donors), the greater relative importance of portfolio management to some nonprofits than to most for-profits, and differences in staff capabilities.

Bearing in mind characteristic differences in attitude (having to do principally with mission) and in the distribution of time and attention across functions, let us now consider in more detail what boards actually do and don't do.

Policy-Making

Perhaps the first point to make is that in both sectors boards almost never "make policy" in any thoroughgoing way, although that is one of the responsibilities frequently ascribed to them. Rather, they raise questions, debate policy, and eventually adopt (or not) recommendations brought to them by the president or CEO. As Katzenbach has observed, the very thought of a board actually making policy, from scratch, is frightening in the extreme. Chaos would surely result. Policies need to be formulated thoughtfully, over time, through the sustained attention of full-time officers and competent staff. "New inspirations" are to be welcomed, but they need to be analyzed carefully outside board meetings, not decided on the spur of the moment.

Boards can, however, improve significantly the making of policy. They can do this, first, by asking the right questions, which are almost never purely financial ones; second, by "making sure that each realistic course of action has been identified and that a good faith stab has been made at weighing the costs and benefits of the main options";[7] and third, by occasionally introducing new approaches. When a board is functioning well, this process is easy, interactive, and iterative. It involves discussions and conversations among board members, the CEO, and perhaps other senior officers, with exchanges of ideas often occurring outside meetings as well as at them. No one is sure, finally, who contributed what, and the seamless nature of the process is itself a compliment to all concerned.

Strategic Planning

In recent years, more boards in both sectors have concentrated on strategic planning, which is all to the good, as long as process is not elevated over substance. There is a risk, which seems to me especially pronounced in the nonprofit sector, that putting numbers in the designated columns, and extrapolating trends, can become a substitute for thinking hard about priorities and hard choices. It is especially important to guard against overly optimistic projections of revenues—a tendency that is also all too common in the public sector.

"Are we on the right track?" "Are there exciting new opportunities to be seized?" Or, as the British ask: "Have we lost our way?" Business boards have a longer history of addressing such questions systematically—which is not to say that they have always found the right answers. The widely publicized problems of companies as different as General Motors, IBM, Eastman Kodak, and American Express (see Appendix B) all relate in one way or another to strategic planning that was either inadequate or wrong in the directions chosen.

IBM is a particularly interesting case because it illustrates so well how difficult these problems can be—how hard it is to know precisely what questions to ask, and then how to assess the answers given. As Charles Exley, the former chairman of NCR has said:

> IBM, in contrast to _____ [another company, which Exley regarded as simply mismanaged], is the victim of a technology revolution which spelled big trouble for the company no matter what they did. When you make the best milk bottle in town [mainframe computers] and someone discovers milk cartons [distributed processing], you confront one huge problem to which there are no easy solutions.

There are also numerous instances in which companies that thought strategically "got it right." To cite an example, in the mid-1980s, Lewis Preston, Dennis Weatherstone, and the board of J.P. Morgan anticipated the declining importance of traditional bank-lending activities and repositioned Morgan for the 1990s by adopting a strategy designed to build up Morgan's ability to compete successfully with the first-tier investment banking firms. In effect, Morgan protected and expanded its franchise as a leading provider of credit to major corporations worldwide by developing a full-blown securities underwriting capability.

More recently, the board of Merck has wrestled hard with fundamental changes in the distribution of prescription drugs, which are occurring at breathtaking speed. The decision to acquire Medco (a leader in managing the costs of pharmaceutical benefits) represents an effort to get at least some distance ahead of the proverbial wave: not simply to wait until the kinds of industrywide changes that have engulfed other companies also deprive Merck of its leadership role in health care, but rather to allow the company to participate effectively in new and irreversible marketing trends. Only time will tell whether this particular acquisition was a good idea, but we must at least give the board (and particularly the CEO, Roy Vagelos) credit for thinking, and acting, strategically.

Nonprofit boards of every kind have also been devoting more attention to the strategic planning aspect of board governance. For example, the New York Public Library developed an elaborate plan predicated on the creation of new space for stacks under Bryant Park, which also involved the establishment of a new center for its business collections and related activities in the B. Altman building.[8] The existence of such a plan, with well-defined financial parameters, appears to have served the library well, especially in the aftermath of the sudden death of its president, Tim Healy. The board of the New York Botanical Garden, in developing its long-term plan, had to make a very different kind of judgment—whether to undertake major investments in the infrastructure needed to attract larger numbers of visitors (such as parking lots and other amenities), all in the hope of increasing earned income significantly.

The extent of board participation in strategic planning varies considerably. A key determinant is the nature of the issues and the expertise that is required, and how well it matches up against the expertise that the board possesses. Michael Blumenthal, now at Lazard Freres and the retired CEO of UNISYS, has suggested that strategic questions for nonprofit organizations such as the New York Botanical Garden do not generally require as much technical sophistication as do strategic questions for a company such as IBM. Relatively few directors are likely to have the background to contribute substantively in an IBM-like environment, whereas more directors will be able to evaluate the desirability of investing in infrastructure at the New York Botanical Garden to raise earned income. (Other types of nonprofits, including hospitals, can face strategic issues that are as complex in their own way as those facing computer companies.)

Perhaps the overriding obligation of boards in both sectors is to require that *a sensible plan of some kind be in place* and that *it be monitored carefully.* It is surprising how frequently no real planning occurs, especially in parts of the nonprofit world. And it is even more surprising how frequently plans that were adopted are not tracked in even the most rudimentary fashion. In several specific situations, it has proved impossible for the staff at the Mellon Foundation, when asked to review grant proposals, to determine whether previously established goals were ever achieved.

This is one respect in which many nonprofits have much to learn from their corporate counterparts, even recognizing that small nonprofits, in particular, lack the staff and other resources to carry out even a simple planning process. Deciding how much an impoverished nonprofit should spend on such efforts is not easy. Board members familiar with planning processes may be of special help in suggesting practical ways of making at least modest progress on this front without large expenditures. More generally, when nonprofit entities do plan, their boards tend to be more intimately involved in the process than are the directors of for-profit companies—in part, as previously suggested, because of the greater apparent accessibility of the questions at issue, and in part because nonprofits are less likely to have a large, highly professionalized internal staff already at work assessing options.

A clear sense of the mission of the institution and a well-thought-out strategic plan can help the boards of nonprofits address one kind of recurring issue peculiar to organizations such as museums, libraries, and historical societies. When should they turn down gifts in kind that are offered "out of the blue"? There are evident dangers in taking on new responsibilities unless there is both a programmatic case for doing so and reason to believe that the resources needed over the long term can be identified. Another of my colleagues, Kevin Guthrie, has suggested that in many cases the wise advice is "Don't Take the Jaguar." His reference was to the game show situation in which a participant wins a Jaguar and may be tempted to take the "free" prize without thinking carefully about what it will cost to maintain the car and pay insurance (never mind the income tax payments to come). Guthrie is now working on a history of the New-York Historical Society that illustrates vividly the degree to which seemingly easy and innocent decisions of this kind can have extraordinary consequences for the long-term welfare of an organization.

Earmarked grants pose analogous issues for nonprofits. Colleges and universities, in particular, regularly confront situations in which donors (often foundations) offer partial or short-term support for a major new program of interest to the prospective donor. Institutions are constantly tempted to move in new directions, sometimes almost without knowing it, by the urge to stay in the vanguard of their fields.

All such decisions to accept matching funds, add programs, create new institutes, and so on, involve judgments concerning what is central to the mission of an institution and what constitutes a distraction. Boards are in a much better position to reach conclusions, and to explain them persuasively to donors and others whom they will not want to offend, if every such "opportunity" can be examined in the context of a well-understood strategic plan. For-profit companies also need to stay focused and to avoid distracting forays and unnecessary entanglements, but they are less likely to face the problem of responding appropriately to offers of "free gifts."

Other Important Board Functions

Legitimizing Policy Decisions

Whatever role boards play in the development of policy and the setting and monitoring of strategic plans, they have a clear-cut responsibility to act on policy recommendations. In both for-profit and nonprofit contexts, votes by boards on major policy issues serve the function of legitimizing decisions and giving them a degree of finality, so the organization can get on with its business. While boards also review and sometimes approve decisions that are more managerial (e.g., salary increases for an array of staff members), a board's role in the policy arena is much more significant.

The very existence of scheduled board meetings, at which recommendations are made and actions taken, has the added virtue of focusing the work of staff members. Materials are prepared more carefully, with greater consideration to potential objections, than would occur in the absence of regular board review. The quality of staff work is—or at least should be—improved as a result of the anticipation of searching questions and critical scrutiny. Also, staff morale improves materially when it is evident that the board is interested in staff members and in listening to what they have to say.

Especially in impecunious nonprofits, where salaries are low and there is little logistical support for even senior staff members, board attention can make a great difference in how people feel about their work. This is one reason it makes sense for staff members to participate in some fashion or other in portions of board meetings.

In some parts of the nonprofit world, boards also can protect a CEO from any tendency to respond too sympathetically to idiosyncratic pressures. One of the responsibilities of a board is to take the long view and to resist actions that serve only to placate some noisy constituency. In some situations, presidents may need to promise individuals (doctors on a hospital staff, key faculty members in a university, or prospective "donors of Jaguars" to museums, for instance) that a matter will be presented to the board, even if the president has a quite certain sense of the likely outcome. In the vernacular, one function of boards is to "take some of the heat."

It should be acknowledged, however, that there are also situations (perhaps at least as numerous) in which boards themselves are sources of strong pressure exerted on behalf of special interests of one kind or another. In a university context, athletics is the most obvious example.* Several commentators have remarked that special pleading by trustees can be a particularly serious problem in the foundation world, especially if a kind of "senatorial courtesy" is allowed to prevail in the absence of strong board leadership. One experienced trustee (John Whitehead) has referred, ruefully, to "pork-barrel reciprocity."

---

*Though by no means the only one. Involved trustees can push relentlessly for support of any number of favorite projects. My most vivid personal recollection along these lines is of a trustee at Princeton who was concerned about the fate of the school's mascot and argued vigorously for dedicating a certain percentage of all Annual Giving receipts to a campaign in India to "Save the Tiger."

Mobilizing Support for Decisions

Boards also exist to mobilize support for decisions taken, especially controversial ones. In nonprofit organizations, this is an absolutely critical function. To cite a lesson growing out of an early experience of mine in the university world, lay members of boards often can be much more effective in defending free speech on a campus (for instance when an unpopular speaker has been invited) than can the president or a dean, who may be thought beholden to the group of faculty or students who invited the speaker or, worse yet, to be the captive of "radical elements."*

Giving Advice to Management

Another important function of boards (or in this context perhaps I should say "members of boards") is to give informal advice to the CEO outside board meetings. A number of commentators regard this as *the* most important function of directors. Anyone who has been responsible for leading a complex organization certainly recognizes the need for advice—and for more *candid* advice from truly knowledgeable and concerned people than is usually available. This is true in both for-profit and nonprofit settings, and I would draw no distinction in this regard. Of course, CEOs must be receptive to advice if it is to have value, and unfortunately those who need advice the most sometimes seem to be the most reluctant to take it.

---

*In 1956, when McCarthyism was a strong force in American society, Alger Hiss spoke on the Princeton campus at the invitation of a student group, thereby bringing a storm of protest down on the head of President Dodds and the university. Fortunately, the board of trustees contained lay members who understood the desirability of letting students (acting wisely or unwisely) invite whomever they chose; and who were willing to defend the essential principles of academic freedom. These lay board members were far more effective than any academic officer could have been in defending the principle at issue. Their success in this regard was attributable in no small measure to their understanding the basic mission of the institution so well.

Remaining Vigilant

Needless to say, giving advice cannot become a substitute for monitoring performance. William T. Allen, chancellor of the Delaware Court of Chancery and a keen student of corporate governance, has expressed this point of view with feeling:

> Men and women who as directors are passive; who view their role as mere advisors; who are pliant and pleasant, but who do not insist upon a real monitor's role, do small service to anyone and deserve little respect.[9]

All boards must evaluate the job being done by their CEOs on a regular basis, make a change if that is called for, and arrange an orderly and effective transition to new leadership at the appropriate time. This can be an excruciatingly painful task, and it is often postponed, if not avoided altogether, in both the for-profit and nonprofit sectors. Much of the discussion of organizational norms (in Chapters 3 and 4) is focused on mechanisms that facilitate or inhibit the proper exercise of this critically important function.

We can all agree, I think, that whatever the exact mix of functions performed by the members of a particular board, service as a director or trustee ought to be serious work—no sinecure. However, the nature and extent of a director's involvement can, and should, vary considerably depending on circumstances. When things are going badly, meetings are likely to be more frequent, discussion more pointed, and decisions harder to make. Extra work is required.

When things are going well, vigilance is the main obligation, and the principal danger is not that directors (or trustees) will do too little, but that, especially in the nonprofit world, some will try to do too much. I recall an occasion at Princeton, during generally good times, when one trustee, perhaps fearful that he was not "doing enough," injected himself into a labor negotiation in such a way as to injure the interests of the institution. It can be hard for active people, many of whom are used to being in charge, to sit back and be satisfied with "just" asking questions. Richard Lyman, who served as president of Stanford from 1970 to 1980, and then as president of the Rockefeller Foundation, observed this same phenomenon and offered this comment:

> I see no way to avoid this problem, unless one purposely fills the board with nonentities and underachievers, but giving plain recognition to the paradox involved in asking movers and shakers to concentrate on their fiduciary responsibilities may help in educating new trustees.

There is never any assurance, however, that meetings will be tranquil and that calm will always prevail. One of the challenges in building a board is to attract individuals who can be both peaceful when that is appropriate and as actively involved as necessary under other conditions. As a former colleague once observed, "Boredom is the price of eternal vigilance."[10] I have been told of an alternative formulation by Aldo Papone (a colleague on the board of American Express): "Directors are like airline pilots, in that their lives consist of hours of boredom, punctuated by moments of terror."

The Role of the Board versus the Role of Management and Staff

Another large set of questions concerns the proper division of duties between board members and management and staff. What is board business and what is not?

At the most basic level, it is easy to say that the board should be concerned with policy and oversight functions, while the staff should be responsible for management and administration. This distinction is not easily drawn in practice, however, and the proper line of demarcation varies across organizations and even within the same organization, depending on circumstances.

The risk of overinvolvement by directors or trustees is greatest, I think, in the case of nonprofit entities—especially when the activities of the organization at least seem relatively simple (well within the grasp of lay board members) and the membership of the board includes donors whom one wishes not to offend. A colleague (Kellum Smith) who has had extensive experience as a trustee of private schools wrote to me as follows:

> Private school boards are composed chiefly of parents, "past parents" (as they tend, amusingly, to be called), and alumni of the school. Typically, the more recent graduates want nearly everything changed; those who were graduated some years ago want nothing changed. Parents, on the other hand, although appropriately obsequious when trying to get their kids into the school and suitably humble when asked to join the board, soon conclude that it is they, as trustees, who are "hiring" the professional staff to run the school and teach their kids; and that, as they learn from their kids what is happening in the school, they are uniquely equipped to judge it. And they may not be wholly successful at distinguishing between the level of detail at which they instruct . . . an employee at the office and the level of detail appropriate to their impulse to affect the substance and manner of teaching. That is not true of all parent or alumni trustees, of course. Some have a keen sense of the distinction between policy and administration and, when they serve on committees such as an "education committee," between an advisory and consultative role and a controlling role. Those are the ones that a good chairman tries to get onto the committees; and a good chairman usually has to expend quite a lot of effort in keeping others off the committees.

There are also situations in which a highly active mode of involvement by trustees seems entirely appropriate. For example, the trustees of the Center for Advanced Study in the Behavioral Sciences make decisions concerning eligibility for fellowships at the Center on a case-by-case basis. Odd as it may sound at first hearing, this procedure seems to me to make sense in this specific context. First, the Center has no permanent faculty and, therefore, there is no internal group of professionals, excepting the director and one or two associates, who could make such decisions; in effect, the board has to function as a faculty. Second, the board of the Center has been constituted in such a way that its members have the professional competence to select fellows. Needless to say, the number of situations in which both conditions are met is severely limited, and that is why the line between board and staff responsibilities is generally drawn quite differently.

As the foregoing discussion suggests, a key variable is the presence of a set of full-time professionals inside an organization judged fully competent to make day-to-day decisions on their own. In considering why boards sometimes manage too much, Dayton has suggested: "Boards always tend to fill management voids."[11] Any temptation by a board to become too involved is much reduced when an organization has within it a large number of officers and staff members with professional standing. This condition is normally satisfied in complex nonprofit institutions as well as in almost all businesses. In such settings, boards are unlikely to involve themselves with "administration" unless they have reason to question the quality of the decisions being made or the integrity of the decision-making process itself. However, when there are serious doubts about the wisdom of what is being done, some checking up is obviously in order.

The serious danger is that a correct sense of proper limits on the intrusiveness of a board under normal circumstances will be used to justify too much detachment when major problems arise. Detailed oversight is required when an organization simply isn't doing well, even if the board has confidence in the management. As one commentator (Taylor Reveley) observed: "No matter how great a board may think an administration is, if the organization begins to head for the rocks, the board's got to intervene to try to help figure out what's wrong."

I am certainly not suggesting that any time an institution gets in trouble, the board should become the management. When close scrutiny is needed, the objective should be not merely to fix some specific malfunction, but to assess the organization's leadership and the reliability of internal processes. If either the leadership or the decision-making process is found wanting, the board should correct the underlying problem. In genuinely serious situations, it is often necessary to find new leadership, or new staff members, to whom responsibility *can* be delegated.

3

How Boards
Are Constituted

I begin this chapter with a confession. For many years, I was contemptuous of the notion that there are compelling principles we should bear in mind in answering practical questions about the operations of a board. And I remain convinced that there are few, if any, formulaic solutions to issues of governance. We should always be ready to hear the case for an exception to anything purporting to be an overriding principle. But experience has taught me that it is possible, even necessary, to have in mind what I call *"presumptive norms"—propositions that should govern the size, composition, structure, and functioning of boards unless there is a convincing case for consciously setting them aside in a particular context.*

I have 20 norms to propose, and for ease of exposition I shall group them under three broad headings:

1. Norms related to *how boards are constituted*—in their size, membership, and composition (including personal qualities, diversity, and independence of directors), terms of service,

and compensation—these norms are the subject of this chapter.

2. Norms related to *how boards are organized*—to the role of the CEO vis-à-vis the board (in part, the "separate chairman" or "lead director" debate), committee structure, frequency and nature of meetings, and succession planning—these norms are covered in Chapter 4.

3. Norms related to *how boards are informed*—to the adequacy of information provided to directors and the need (especially in the nonprofit sector) for "key indicators"—these norms are discussed in Chapter 5.

Although presented one by one, these 20 norms are interrelated and should be considered together.

Size

1 | **The size of for-profit boards should normally fall within a range of, say, 10 to 15 members; many nonprofit boards should be larger—in the range of, say, 12 to 30, with even larger sizes justified in some circumstances.**

There is widespread agreement that a board's capacity to perform its functions is critically dependent on its size. While there is nothing magical about any particular number, boards can be both too small and too large. There are numerous examples of problems at both extremes. Although skillful leadership and careful management of board affairs can mitigate these problems, there is no escaping the fact that size itself matters greatly.

Drawbacks of Small Boards

At the bottom end of the usual ranges, a board with fewer than 10 or 12 members runs the risk of being insufficiently diverse in the range of backgrounds, experiences, and perspectives that it encompasses.

Also, very small boards can be overly dependent on one or two people to contribute certain talents, a particular perspective, or a distinctive style (both feisty critics and conciliators are needed). Even exceptionally dedicated board members will miss an occasional meeting because of illness or conflicts, and such absences can be debilitating if the board is so small that it contains no backups. Finally, smaller boards naturally provide fewer candidates to serve in leadership positions—to chair committees, if not the board itself and, in the case of nonprofits, to lead fund-raising campaigns.

Grant-making foundations are a revealing exception to assumptions about the appropriate size of nonprofit boards. They tend to be appreciably smaller. The Council on Foundations has reported that average board size is now 10.3, having increased from 9.5 in 1988 and 9.9 in 1990.[1] Perhaps one reason is that these foundations do not normally solicit contributions and therefore do not need to make room on their boards for potential donors or fund raisers. Grant-making foundations also have no need to recruit students, attract audiences, or seek clients; thus, their constituencies are less diverse.

Drawbacks of Very Large Boards

It is even clearer that boards can be too large to function effectively. It is obviously far harder to achieve a genuinely interactive mode of discussion and decision making when the board becomes too large. One experienced CEO (Michael Blumenthal) articulated a widely held view:

> Twelve-to-fifteen is best for most corporate boards. Certainly at 18–24, real group cohesion, interaction, debate and collegiality become impossible—in my experience at least.

Boards can be too large for individual accountability to survive. Beyond some limit, it becomes easy for individual members to be anonymous—to defer, de facto, to others. When all members of a large group are thought to be equally responsible, no one may feel really responsible. One board member (John Whitehead) offered the candid observation: "I find that there is an inverse correlation between the size of a board and my sense of responsibility to it."

The far more serious problem, in any case, is boards that are so large their size compromises effective governance:

> . . . As a rule, if there are more than . . . 24 members, the sheer size of the board erodes its effectiveness. Members can shelter poor attendance, lack of preparation, avoidance of difficult issues and failing to do anything significant *amid the heaving mass of the board* [emphasis added].[2]

There is evidence of at least some movement in the direction of paring the sizes of overly large nonprofit boards. For example, the American Lung Association is reported to have reduced the size of its boards to 27 members from as many as 130, and the American Association of Museums plans to cut its board to 21 from 75.[3]

It is also noteworthy, and somewhat troubling, that two nonprofit entities which have had more than their share of publicized difficulties, Empire Blue Cross and United Way (see Appendix B), have recently increased the sizes of their boards, which were already, one would have thought, at the limits of workability. The Empire board has grown from 20 to 25 members, and the United Way board has grown from 37 to 45. In both cases, new board members appear to have been added in response to criticisms of board inattentiveness and failure to represent important constituencies. I am in no position to judge the merits of the new appointments, which may all be outstanding. But I do wonder how much consideration was given to "retiring" other directors to make the overall sizes of the boards more consistent with the evident need for disciplined oversight of operations.

Average Sizes of For-Profit and Nonprofit Boards

In the case of for-profit boards, 14 or 15 seems to be a reasonable upper limit. According to one survey, the average size of U.S. corporate boards was 12 in 1991, having declined from 14 in 1987.[4]

Nonprofit boards tend to be larger—*much* larger in some cases. While we have been unable to find any overall survey of board size for charitable nonprofits that would be comparable to the surveys in the corporate sector, a combination of data for orchestras, an informal analysis we have made of our own grantees, and anecdotal information leaves no doubt as to the general picture. The American Symphony Orchestra League found that board size varied directly with the level of annual expenditures, with the number of voting members increasing from an average of 19 for orchestras with annual expenditures below $100,000 to 60 for the orchestras with annual expenditures in excess of $9.9 million. In addition, orchestra boards included an average of 5 to 10 nonvoting members, bringing the overall average for the largest orchestras to 70.[5] A member of the Mellon Foundation's staff (Margaret McKenna) examined the lists of board members of our new grantees in arts and culture, education and scholarship, population, and public affairs for the years 1990–1993. She found that the median size of these nonprofit boards was about 20—a number significantly higher than the average for business boards, but significantly lower than the comparable figure for orchestras.

There are two reasons why nonprofit boards are often large. First, many have to satisfy a wider range of constituencies than do for-profit boards; therefore, they are likely to have a greater need for diversity. Colleges are a good example. As is true of other types of boards, they need a broad range of professional perspectives (business, legal, and investment at the minimum), as well as educational. In addition, they need to reflect the diversity of their student and alumni populations. The board of the American University of Beirut (AUB), which has 30 members, illustrates a further dimension of this reason for large size, in that it needs to have diverse representation from *both* the Middle East and the American continent.

A second consideration is the need to include major donors and those able to solicit contributions on the boards of many nonprofit organizations. Clear tradeoffs are made: Some boards knowingly become larger than they believe they should be because of the high priority given to fund-raising.

Approaches to Limiting the Size of Boards

In an attempt to satisfy fund-raising needs without enlarging their boards too much, some nonprofits make skillful use of "development councils," "advisory boards," and similar mechanisms. While such parallel structures can definitely help (especially if care is taken to make their meetings challenging intellectually), they are rarely a full solution. Some people will be satisfied with nothing less than a seat on the one organizational entity that has power—or, perhaps more important yet, prestige, which tends to be highly correlated with power. Also, coordinating the activities of two complementary instrumentalities is no easy task, as presidents of Harvard University will attest. (Harvard has a small "corporation" with decision-making power and a large "board of overseers," which is advisory.)

The formation and active use of an executive committee is another common way of addressing the problem of size. I am told that this approach has worked well in a number of cases, including the American Academy in Rome and the International Rescue Committee. While there is always the danger that some trustees not on the Executive Committee will feel that they have been consigned to the second tier of a two-tiered board, skillful leadership, candor, and good humor can go a long way toward easing such sensitivities.

The Memorial Sloan-Kettering Cancer Center has developed an even more subtle approach that deserves wider consideration. Its annual report contains a list of about 50 to 55 "members of the Boards of Overseers and Managers." No distinction is made between these two groups. Thus, all of these individuals can say, and believe, that they serve on "the board." At the same time, real decision-making authority rests with the Board of Managers (a "supervisory board," as one person described it), which consists of about 25 individuals who meet six times a year. The Board of Overseers joins with the Board of Managers three times annually and serves in an advisory capacity. The Board of Managers has a committee structure, and Overseers are asked occasionally to serve on various committees of the Board of Managers.

Membership and Composition

Inside Directors*

2 Inside directors can be highly valuable members of boards, and the CEO should not be the only insider; but the number of insiders should be strictly limited—outside directors should predominate.

The relative number of inside directors on corporate boards is reported to have declined from an average of four to an average of three over the past five years.[6] This seems to me a proper shift in the balance of board membership because it strengthens the role of the outside directors. One former CEO (Richard Furlaud) has emphasized the constraints on inside directors:

---

*An "inside director" is defined as a board member who is also a member of management. Boards may also include directors who have other business relationships with the company (see norm 6).

> Insiders can never be influential board members in their own right. They simply must vote with the CEO. They can serve other important functions, but they cannot be counted on to exert any real independence.

For this reason, a specific limit on the number of inside directors is appropriate, and the general consensus seems to favor a maximum of three or four, with many commentators favoring just two (the CEO and one other management person).

While I am a strong proponent of a truly independent board and agree that insiders should constitute a distinct minority of board members, this is one area in which I think there is some danger of overcompensating for past sins. For instance, the most recent SpencerStuart Board Index notes that at 14 of the 100 boards that constitute its index, the CEO is now the only inside director—and the report appears to applaud this trend.[7]

In my view, having some insiders on a corporate board, beyond just the CEO, can serve a number of extremely valuable functions:

- Inside directors can provide useful information and new insights. This can be especially important on boards that require technical sophistication and yet are precluded from appointing the most knowledgeable outsiders by conflicts of interest and antitrust laws. Informal relationships between inside and outside directors can facilitate substantive exchanges of ideas by establishing peer relationships and, as one person put it, "encouraging less stilted conversations."
- Succession planning is helped when directors have regular opportunities to evaluate leading contenders in a board setting.
- The election of key management personnel to a board is an indication of their importance. Giving carefully selected individuals a "privileged relationship" with the board can be

decisive in strengthening their allegiance to the company and, therefore, in reducing the likelihood that they will be tempted by outside offers.

Harold Shapiro summarizes well the basic arguments for inside directors:

> The appointment of an internal director gives that person a great deal more independence and may force the CEO to focus on team building rather than "right of command." . . . It also breaks the CEO's monopoly on information and interpretation of strategic developments. I have had experience both ways and very much prefer a board with at least one-third internal directors. In my experience this makes the entire board much better informed.

In the case of nonprofits, it is rare for any insider, other than the president or CEO, to serve as a voting member of the board, though arrangements are often made for key individuals to meet regularly with the board and sometimes to serve in nonvoting capacities. This structural difference is rooted in distinctive organizational structures (there is less hierarchy in most nonprofits, and less likelihood of promotion to CEO from within). The presence of inside directors is simply much less of an issue.

Personal Qualities

3 | **Selection of exceptional individuals to serve as outside directors is of paramount importance, and courage and empathy are key qualities that should be emphasized.**

Effective governance by any board surely depends, most of all, on having an outstanding group of members. The right people can make any structure work, and no structure can be so brilliantly conceived that it will compensate for inadequacies of individuals.

I have little to add to the usual catalog of virtues to be borne in mind in selecting board members. Integrity, competence, insight, independence, and dedication are obviously necessary, as is the ability to work with colleagues in a setting that requires collective decision making. But I will advance one other proposition in which I have come to believe strongly: *Courage and the will to act are often the attributes in scarcest supply.* In my experience, after some amount of time and discussion (to be sure, frequently too much time and too much discussion), what should be done usually becomes fairly clear. The trick is marshaling the energy—and especially the courage—to act. It is so much easier simply to wait a little longer for events to unfold.

Unfortunately, the problem is deeper than merely finding individuals with the requisite backbone, though that is, I suspect, the largest part of it. The more subtle and less tractable problem is related to what Lewis Bernard has described perceptively as "the Director's Dilemma:"

> Executive management must be left free to run the company uninhibited by excessive interference by the board. The issue, of course, is what is excessive interference? I find that most conscientious directors are overly shy about being perceived as rocking the boat. This leads to a broader question. Can directors be more than a purely *reactive* force? The catch-22 is that the reluctance to be perceived as interfering makes for passive rather than active board participants. The importance of not engaging or interfering in short-term management frequently causes directors to abdicate their responsibility for long-term direction. The "director's dilemma" is a difficult one; I suspect you may have felt it acutely at times.

Another commentator, who exceeds any normal standard of conscientiousness and courage (David Culver, chairman of CAI Capital Corporation and retired chairman of ALCAN Aluminium Ltd.) starts from what he calls "General Doriot's definition of an organization as a group of individuals helping one person do a job." In his view, directors are there to help the CEO do what is assuredly a most difficult job, and therein lies the problem. Culver's further comments are insightful:

> There is no problem as long as the organization is, as you say, "on a roll." But then along comes the day when the CEO, barely disguising his adrenalin, proposes a big bold move. He has done his best to keep his board informed. He has made it abundantly clear to the other party—and to his staff—that the matter is subject to board approval, etc., etc. As a director, you don't like it. It doesn't feel right. However, it is a fast-moving world, and if I say "no way," I am pulling the rug out from under the feet of the person I am trying to help "do a job." Thus the director finds himself making comments about the proposed deal—knowing that it is too late to stop it from happening (the other 80% of the board is not going to do anything!)—and yet hoping to have an influence on the CEO's next idea, not knowing what that next idea could possibly be! It's the essence of indirect influence, not easy to do, and not much fun.
>
> This kind of thing can only go on for so long (usually a whole lot longer than it should—especially in retrospect). Finally, the director has to overrule General Doriot, and conclude that Governance has become the number one priority. New leadership is mandatory.

It is, to be sure, very hard to know when simply raising questions, and eyebrows, is insufficient. Culver is right in suggesting that being effective, without prematurely "pulling the rug," requires artistry of a high order. Perhaps all that we can hope to accomplish, realistically, is to increase the chances that such artistry will be exercised. Two innocent-sounding but surprisingly difficult steps are required:

- The appointment of individuals who have the will to act when conditions require action.

- The creation of a climate and the setting up of structures that will facilitate, rather than inhibit, courageous decision making.

Much of the rest of this book is intended to serve these limited, but important, purposes. The theme introduced here, of the delicate relationship between independent directors and the CEO, is pursued throughout the following pages.

Another, quite different, barrier to the exercise of courage is likely to be felt especially keenly by conscientious directors of nonprofits. It was explained to me by one trustee, known to have courage aplenty, in terms of the reasons even a normally outspoken person might fail to speak up to correct a problem. In serving on boards, this trustee (Taylor Reveley) said he always felt a responsibility to fix problems that he identified. But leading a revolt or making a very pointed comment could precipitate a need for remedial action that he might not have the time or energy to undertake. In such situations, even a courageous person might well remain mute—another reason an undistinguished status quo may remain in place too long.

As these observations remind us, the shortage of *time* is a major problem for many directors—who, seeking to do good, are often tempted to take on more responsibilities than it is reasonable for anyone to assume. There are innumerable stories of exceedingly able individuals who accept board memberships and then attend meetings infrequently if at all. Another practice is for overcommitted individuals to "come late and leave early," or to spend the better part of a meeting on the telephone.

Two rules seem to be accepted in the abstract, though not always honored in practice:

- Expectations concerning the time required to serve on a board should be discussed explicitly when a nomination is being considered.

- No one should be nominated, or agree to be nominated, who cannot make the necessary time available.

There also seems to be agreement that, as we look ahead, greater time commitments will be required of board members, especially those who serve on major corporate boards. It is possible that individual directors and corporate boards in general may develop an informal understanding (perhaps even a "norm") concerning the number of for-profit boards on which busy individuals can serve. A rigid rule—never mind a legal proscription—would be foolish, since individual capabilities and circumstances vary so much, but there could be a general presumption against service on more than, say, three or four major corporate boards. Some commentators believe that two would be a better guideline.

Empathy and Commitment to the Organization's Mission

In choosing members of nonprofit boards another critical attribute is sometimes overlooked or undervalued in composing boards: *a genuine understanding of the mission of the organization, combined with empathy and commitment.* Ron Daniel, former managing director of McKinsey and Company and an active trustee of nonprofit entities as well as an avid student of their behavior, regards this qualification as just as important for nonprofits as courage is in the case of for-profits.

The boards of nonprofit organizations may include individuals who, while highly competent in some general sense, "simply don't get it"—who lack understanding and empathy, who fail to understand how a ballet company functions, how graduate education relates to undergraduate education in a research university, and so on. Daniel's blunt assessment is: "Such a person will never be of any use." People with no visceral "feel" for the organization may be clumsy, behaving in an elephant-like manner and doing real damage, or so insecure that they just do not participate.*

The need for understanding and empathy is one reason nonprofits are ill-advised simply to collect "names" on their boards. Another reason is that some (by no means all) high-profile individuals may feel a need to "perform" at board meetings. When individuals join boards to "make a splash" or advance a personal agenda, the effects can be quite disruptive. Time can be wasted and opportunities for serious discussion of serious matters can be lost. Indeed, the overall character of board meetings can be affected drastically by self-promotion and unfocused contentiousness.

Efforts to democratize processes for choosing members of boards of organizations such as colleges and universities can contribute (inadvertently) to this problem. When trustees are elected from slates, there is a natural tendency for the electorate to choose individuals who sound "interesting," but who may or may not be the most useful board members. The obverse difficulty is that electorates are unlikely to select the steady, dedicated individuals who are needed to anchor every board. While there is much to be said for mechanisms that provide for some amount of direct participation in the selection of trustees by, say, the graduates of a college or university, it is even more important that the board itself retain the authority to fill a clear majority of the places. (Board selection, and the role of nominating committees, is discussed further in Chapter 4.)

4 | The board of every organization should contain several outside directors with particular knowledge of its genre.

---

*Alan Pifer, former president of the Carnegie Corporation and of the Carnegie Foundation for the Advancement of Teaching, told me of a situation in which an otherwise outstanding person was ineffective in chairing the board of a troubled educational institution because he lacked any empathy for faculty members, who were, to be sure, behaving in a most irritating way, but who had to be understood and dealt with nonetheless.

In constructing boards, there is a special need for members who are knowledgeable about the characteristic functions and problems of the particular enterprise in question. While this norm may seem obvious, I highlight it because of its implications for the flow of information. Knowledgeable individuals play a critically important role in helping the board as a whole ask key questions that otherwise might not be posed.

This norm almost always appears to be satisfied on corporate boards because of the presence of other CEOs who have current experience with the same (or similar) problems in their own companies. Having believed this myself, I was somewhat taken aback by several commentators who warned me not to exaggerate the extent to which CEOs will in fact understand another business. Technical content is an important variable, and it may be no accident that three commentators making this general point all chose IBM as their example.

Ironically, antitrust laws and customs in the United States frequently preclude having the most knowledgeable individuals as directors. These are the people who have the most relevant business experience precisely because they are either customers or near-competitors. The Japanese model is at the other end of the spectrum; their boards generally include executives of related firms. Several commentators have suggested that this question should be rethought in the U.S. context. One person observed that the present legal prohibition in the United States against conflicts is yet another argument for having some insiders on the board—they, at least, should understand the technical side of the business and be in a better position to focus board discussion on long-term options and issues.

In the case of nonprofits, "amateurs" are more likely to dominate board rosters. That can be fine, since what is needed is not numerical supremacy, so long as there are at least some board members who have sufficient experience with the particular organizational universe to be alert to new developments, probable traps, and key conventions—who, in short, will know enough to give good advice and raise awkward questions. Important as empathy is, it is no substitute for professional sophistication.

Nonprofits also use board selection processes to recruit a range of professional talent of other kinds that they neither need on a full-time basis nor could afford if it were not volunteered. Investors and lawyers, for example, often fall into this category.

More generally, I believe that every individual on a board should have some special competence or experience to contribute. While it is obviously desirable to have individuals with breadth, it is dangerous, in my view, to recruit people who make careers of serving only as outside directors. Having a deep root in another organization or in a particular vocation is at least partial protection against a kind of dilettantism, and against the danger that individuals who spend too much time serving on boards may be tempted simply to "go through the motions."

To end this section on a rather different note, I am persuaded that another qualification, not really "professional," should be taken seriously in composing boards. It is enormously important to include individuals who make it stimulating and enjoyable—fun—for other directors to come to meetings. The pleasure to be derived from having interesting colleagues is an important reward for service, and the presence of such people encourages fuller attendance and more active participation in the work of the board. This attribute of board membership is a more important determinant of effective governance than most people realize.

Any number of individuals come to mind as illustrations of this point, including the late Malcolm Forbes, the former publisher of *Forbes Magazine*. As many will attest, Mr. Forbes was a wonderfully engaging, irreverent spirit who had the capacity to make even the dreariest occasion interesting. His liveliness never detracted, however, from the serious issues of the day; rather, it served to highlight them and to direct energy to the search for solutions to the most mundane problems. He took his responsibilities as a board member very seriously and could never be regarded as contributing only a "name."

Diversity

5 | Diversity of both backgrounds and perspectives is important in composing a board, but it needs to be achieved without sacrificing agreement on a common set of assumptions about the institution and its mission.

Having an effective board involves not only recruiting exceptional individuals who are well suited to the requirements of the particular organization but also assembling a group of people who complement one another by contributing a variety of backgrounds, experiences, and perspectives. For example, boards of colleges and universities must be diverse if they are to be effective as questioners and decision makers, if their policy decisions are to be perceived as "responsible" and "legitimate," and if they are to be successful in appealing for support from the institution's varied constituencies. When such boards discuss the implications of requirements of gender equity for athletic programs, it is obviously desirable to have the participation of women as well as men. Similarly, discussion of the contentious issue of how to handle racial slurs in the context of an institution's commitment to free speech will benefit from the participation of trustees who are members of minority groups.

For many organizations, no problem is more difficult at the present time than finding the best way of including on governing boards members of previously excluded groups, especially racial minorities. It can be tempting to adopt the easy approach of earmarking positions (the "black seat" on a board), but this seems to me patronizing, potentially very dangerous, and an inadequate response to the *opportunity* to enrich a board by recruiting outstanding individuals of diverse backgrounds and persuasions.

Without discussing the large and important subject of diversity in detail, I will advance one proposition: *It is undesirable for a board to be limited to "one of anything," even though practical constraints on size preclude giving full effect to this "Noah's Ark" principle.* It is much easier, for example, for women and members of minority groups to address the full range of issues presented to a board from their individual perspectives if the board is not expecting a single woman, or a single member of a minority group, somehow to present *the* perspective of women or minorities—as if any such thing as a single perspective existed in the first place. Similarly, it may be better if there is more than one corporate CEO (assuming that no respectable board would have none!) and more than one educator, too. The general point is that overlapping backgrounds and experiences allow boards to hear a more nuanced set of opinions, and to calibrate these opinions with greater precision. While limits on the size of boards constrain the ability to satisfy this objective fully, it should be kept in mind in filling vacancies.

We should, I believe, reject categorically any notion that individual members "represent" particular constituencies. The case for diversity should not be construed this way. If individuals believe they are on a board to represent a particular group, or a particular point of view, they will not be what Quakers call "weighty" board members. It is too easy to dismiss their arguments as special pleading. To have influence, individuals must think for themselves and be perceived by others as concerned about the best interests of the organization as a whole. This simple proposition cuts in many directions. Just as it would be wrong to expect minority group members to speak for "their group," it would be just as wrong for other board members to feel that they have no responsibility to be sensitive to such concerns because others are assumed to feel them more acutely.

Central to my thinking is the need to achieve diversity without losing essential commonalities. As one person put it: "All board members must believe in certain things [the basic mission of the organization, especially] or it will be impossible for the board to function." Stories abound of well-intentioned efforts to diversify boards that unfortunately ended up by frustrating everyone concerned. Backgrounds, life-styles, and modes of discourse can become so heterogeneous that it is impossible, as a practical matter, for informed and focused discussion to occur. In such situations, people lose patience.

One former staff member described the experiences of a foundation in the late 1960s and 1970s this way:

> What I observed was not merely a loss of collegiality but a loss of the capacity to deliberate in an orderly way and to reach genuine consensus on shared objectives. Old-line board members mingled an exaggerated respect for the (to them) exotic life experiences of the newcomers with mystification at much that they were saying. The old-line board members' reluctance to press for clarification and precision (for fear of seeming rude or overbearing) resulted in some very peculiar and, I think, ill-thought-out decisions. In my opinion, those decisions not only diminished the effectiveness of the institution but resulted in general board dissatisfaction. . . . Many of the newcomers with agendas (and many of them had been chosen precisely because they were known to have them) were rarely able to feel that their agendas had been endorsed as fully or warmly as they felt they should be. Other board members felt that an assortment of agendas had been foisted on them without that degree of arrived-at joint conviction that had traditionally accompanied board decisions. . . . Some lost interest in board service. . . . Consensus became simply impossible, being replaced by factionalism, rancorous dispute, and decision by ballot.

This sad account may be somewhat overstated, but I suspect it is accurate enough to alert us to large potholes in the road. Seeking diversity certainly need not have these effects, and in most cases has not had. A practical way of increasing the odds that a truly diverse board will work together effectively involves recruiting individuals who are familiar with the workings of complex organizations and have participated in the leadership of such organizations, preferably at reasonably high levels. Generally speaking, board members who have the most difficulty functioning effectively are those who simply do not understand how boards work, the pressures under which a CEO labors, the need to achieve consensus, and so on—usually because they have had no opportunity to learn these things. Direct experience as a front-line manager has the great virtue of educating potential board members about the humbling compromises that must be made in moving from an idea to a practical result.

I recognize that emphasizing such experience restricts pools of candidates and, in a nontrivial sense, reduces the diversity that can be achieved. I do not favor making such a criterion absolute. Among other things, talented individuals must be allowed to "start somewhere," and boards have some obligation to provide opportunities that will prove educational to the individuals concerned. The presence of other board members with leadership experience will help this process while simultaneously allowing the board as a whole to function better.

The preceding comments, with the exception of the last two paragraphs, have been written almost entirely from the perspective of nonprofit boards. While corporate boards have also become more diverse (more women now serve and there is also a greater presence of minority group members), no one has suggested that they run any risk of becoming "too diverse." A far more common problem, according to the testimony of many, is the need to achieve enough genuine diversity of views (by no means the same thing as having "x" women and "y" minority members on the board) to guard against what has been called "groupthink," defined as:

> . . . A mode of thinking that people engage in when they are deeply involved in a cohesive in-group, when the members' striving for unanimity overrides their motivation to realistically appraise alternative courses of action. . . . Groupthink refers to a deterioration of mental efficiency, reality testing, and moral judgment that results from in-group pressures. . . . The more amiability and esprit de corps among the members of a policy-making in-group, the greater is the danger that independent critical thinking will be replaced by groupthink.[8]

It is surprising how easy it can be for a closely knit board to come to major decisions without really considering major risks and potentially adverse consequences. Needless to say, this can happen in both the nonprofit and for-profit sectors.

Diversity is one antidote to this malady. I continue to believe that collegiality can be strengthened, not weakened, by the honest exchange of a variety of well-considered viewpoints.

Independence

6 | **In selecting board members, care should be taken to avoid "incestuous" relationships and to preserve a certain amount of distance between board members and the CEO.**

In this respect, as in so many others, there is no substitute, finally, for good judgment, which is why it is possible to state this norm pertaining to the independence of board members in only the most general terms. Donald Perkins is surely right in saying: "Independence for a director is an attitude."[9] Still, some proscriptions, or at least presumptions, can be useful in protecting against perceived conflicts.

Conflicts of Interest

Perhaps the most obvious injunction is that the CEO should not serve on the compensation committee of any board led by another member of his own board—a mixing of relationships that inevitably raises questions about the ability of the board member to evaluate the performance of the CEO on the merits. A more sweeping proscription, with which I agree, is that CEOs should not serve in *any* capacity on each other's boards.

Another delicate subject is the presence on a board of individuals who work for organizations that have major business relationships with the company in question. Some commentators have raised questions about the independence of investment bankers as directors. Similar questions can be raised concerning the presence on boards of partners in law firms that represent the company, employees of vendors, and so on. While individuals can, and no doubt usually do, rise above such potential conflicts and act with integrity, more and more weight is being given, and should be given, to appearances—to the desirability of not putting either individual members or a board as a whole in awkward situations. Several commentators advocated a firm rule against *any* business relationships between a company and entities with "representatives" on its board.[10] The related issue raised when board members serve a company simultaneously as directors and consultants is discussed later in this chapter when we consider compensation.

Excess Loyalty

A more insidious danger, because it is less visible, is that boards will include individuals tied too closely together—and too closely to the CEO—by other loyalties, which can be political or purely personal. One commentator referred to "insidious social links" and another to the consequences of "club-like" relationships.

The consequences can be serious. In the words of Michael Blumenthal:

> The sense of honor, prestige, and importance people derive from certain types of board service is not to be underrated. You certainly know that from Princeton and it applies to many persons who serve on the most prestigious corporate boards as well. . . . It helps your standing in the business community to be a director of, say, GE, GM, IBM, etc. That also means that, once inducted into the most prestigious "club," it inhibits asking the nasty questions. You want to *stay* a member! It's tough to be the skunk at the garden party (I know!). All that is very much part of the group dynamic of "going along."

This is tricky territory because long associations and friendships can contribute to the effective functioning of organizations. Personal relationships often lead people to devote more time and attention to the task at hand than they would otherwise; also, friends are sometimes more willing to raise hard questions early on, before a crisis erupts, and to be more direct in their criticisms, than "acquaintances," who may fear that comments will be misunderstood or motives questioned. There is no way to legislate against this potential barrier to independent decision making without simultaneously sacrificing advantages worth more than whatever protection against possible abuse can be purchased by strict rules. Sensitivity is what is required.

Dennis Weatherstone, chairman and CEO of J.P. Morgan, has suggested that *retired* CEOs are often able to provide a good mixture of friendship or familiarity and independence. To at least some degree, retired CEOs have "left the club." For that reason, they may feel less inhibited than active CEOs: freer to speak up, to take unpopular positions, and even to seek the resignation of the CEO when that seems necessary. Weatherstone suggests that it is more than coincidence that in three of the most widely publicized board eruptions (GM, American Express, and Eastman Kodak), retired CEOs (Smale, Warner, and Phelan, respectively) provided strong leadership within their respective boards.

It would also help if all participants in the governance process would acknowledge more openly and explicitly that there is an inescapable tension between maintaining distance and maintaining trust and collegiality. Both are important, and a sensible balance must be struck. No one should be surprised or offended if the need for board members to be simultaneously supportive and critical creates some continuing uneasiness. It should. This is, after all, the essence of the "director's dilemma" discussed earlier.

Nonprofit Board Policies

Conflicts of interest are present in the nonprofit world too, where they can be just as troubling. It is tempting for board members to suggest that their firms provide business services to nonprofits, often (though certainly not always) out of the most altruistic motives. Nonprofits are subject to the same risks as for-profits that personal friendships and social or political relationships will influence judgments of board members. Moreover, it can be very awkward to terminate a business relationship—for example, with a money management firm—when the service-providing organization is led by a board member. Grant-making foundations must also be concerned about their relationships with grant-seekers identified with board members.

For all these reasons, nonprofits have increasingly adopted written standards, sometimes tailored to their own circumstances. To illustrate, the trustees of the Mellon Foundation have just adopted a statement, "The Appearance of Private Benefit," which went through numerous drafts and stimulated much debate. There was no disagreement on the objectives to be served, but it was far from easy to find phraseology that captured the spirit of the discussion. The more we talked, the clearer it became that rigid proscriptions would do more harm than good, particularly when we left the relatively straightforward domain of purely business relationships (where the usual standards seemed just as appropriate for the Foundation as for any for-profit organization) and entered the realm of grant-making. The board could have adopted a policy that precluded grants to any organization headed by a trustee, but decided not to do so.

The implications of such a policy for the Foundation's program in higher education show why such a policy seemed unwise. The Foundation has always had distinguished university presidents on its board, and the guidance of these individuals has been enormously helpful in fashioning programs that reach across broad sectors of higher education. If the Foundation were unable to make grants to the colleges or universities led by these presidents, such academics would have no alternative but to resign from the board in order to protect the interests of their institutions. Other presidents would also be unwilling to serve, and the Foundation would be deprived of the help of precisely the set of people best positioned to give informed advice. There are other ways to protect against potential conflicts (including full disclosure and abstention from votes) without excessive sacrifices of talent needed by the board.

Efforts of this kind seem to me highly desirable, and not only because of the evident importance of avoiding the improper exercise of influence. The very process of debating what rules make sense for a particular organization can heighten sensitivities and prevent potential problems from arising in the future.

Presence of Former CEOs on Boards

7 | A former CEO should not continue to serve on the board, except in rare cases and (at most) for a short time.

It is evident that retaining the services of the former CEO on the board has advantages. Key relationships with investors, customers, and donors can be maintained. Historical knowledge—"institutional memory"—is available to the board. The benefits of continuity are maximized. Moreover, as examples of exemplary behavior indicate, a sensitive person can handle, with style as well as judgment, the inevitable ambiguities growing out of such a shift in roles. Nonetheless, the arguments against continuing service on the board are stronger.

It is important to recall that all these norms are presumptions, not ironbound rules. The "rare cases" in which it can make sense for a retiring CEO to stay on a board include situations in which the newly elected CEO needs, and wants, some transitional help. A danger, however, in opening the door at all for exceptions is that the wrong individuals may step through it. A wise commentator (Arjay Miller) observed that a perverse pattern may develop because, in his words: "The CEOs who would be okay as continuing members of the board do not usually want to stay, whereas the CEOs who want to stay on the board after their retirement are the very ones who should leave."

This set of principles is illustrated by an experience of mine when I first became president of Princeton. I could not understand why it made sense to deprive the board (and me) of the wisdom of my illustrious predecessor, Robert Goheen. He would have been a fine board member and a source of help rather than difficulty for me—but, consistent with Arjay Miller's dictum, he did not want to stay on. In retrospect, I now believe that the members of the Princeton board who (in company with President Goheen) thought it better for me to start off on my own, were right.

A major advantage of a clean break, in both the for-profit and nonprofit worlds, is precisely that it makes clear to one and all that the new CEO is in fact in charge, and fully accountable. As we have seen recently in the corporate context, it can be impossible, especially in contentious situations, to make that central point effectively so long as the former CEO continues to serve on the board. This is a major reason that so much pressure was put on Jim Robinson to resign when Harvey Golub was elected president and CEO of American Express.

There are also other reasons not to keep the former CEO on the board. With the best will in the world, it is hard for any former CEO to be entirely objective about decisions made on his watch. Moreover, friends of the former CEO, and others who do not want to hurt feelings or give offense, will inevitably find it more difficult to raise questions about the need to reverse direction, or modify earlier judgments, if the architect of those decisions, for whom the questioner has both affection and respect, is sitting right across the table.

Two commentators on an early draft of this book, both former CEOs, spoke with feeling on this subject. Michael Blumenthal wrote:

> I absolutely agree that a former CEO should not be on the board. Such a person, even a very good one, can be in an impossible bind. If he criticizes the new incumbent, he is suspect. If he has real reservations and *doesn't* speak out, he is not doing his job. Save him that dilemma. Also, the new CEO is bound to be a bit embarrassed to reverse policies in front of his old boss, particularly if they remain good friends.

The other former CEO echoed these sentiments, with special reference to his own experience. He agreed strongly that retiring CEOs should leave the board. In retrospect, he said that he had:

> . . . made a big mistake in staying on the board after stepping down as CEO. . . . The discussions were painful, I never knew when I should comment or when I should stay quiet, and it was just not a good idea to stay there. If people wanted my views, they could obtain them in other ways.

One wonders about the effects of Roger Smith's continued presence on the General Motors board (from which he has recently retired). And it is no reflection at all on Frank Cary or John Opel to ask whether IBM would have had an easier time changing strategic directions in response to changed conditions if they had not continued to serve as directors. There is widespread agreement that the 1990s are different from the 1980s in innumerable respects, and the case for having an unfettered opportunity to discuss new directions is therefore stronger than ever before. Kotter and Haskett of the Harvard Business School are right, in my view, in emphasizing the importance of the "adaptability of [corporate] cultures"—and in suggesting the advantages of an "outsider" perspective. Retaining the former CEO on the board can rarely be expected to enhance "adaptability."[11]

Also, as already noted, the advice and help of the retired CEO can be obtained absent a board relationship. In the case of the Mellon Foundation, my predecessor, Jack Sawyer, never hesitates to provide helpful advice, while being scrupulously careful to give me full freedom of action. Similarly, Bob Goheen was always ready to do anything I asked him to do at Princeton. There are many comparable examples in the corporate world. In appropriate circumstances, such contributions can be recognized by making former CEOs honorary directors and inviting them to occasional social functions. Some retired CEOs count directors among their closest friends, and this approach has the advantage of acknowledging such friendships in an acceptable way.

To the best of my knowledge, there has been no systematic study of the frequency with which former CEOs have continued to serve as directors in either the for-profit or nonprofit sector. There is little doubt, however, that the characteristic patterns are entirely different. Corporate CEOs have generally been encouraged to stay on boards and often have done so. Retiring presidents of nonprofit organizations, on the other hand, have only rarely continued as trustees of their organizations.

I suspect that this difference in customary practice is attributable mainly to fundamental differences in purposes, internal modes of organization (especially degrees of hierarchy and normal patterns of succession), and distinctive processes of historical evolution. These broad factors are discussed further in Chapter 4, when we consider pervasive differences in the relationship between the positions of CEO and board chairman in the two sectors.

But it is also true that rewards—and "penalties"—for continued service on boards by retired CEOs are not at all the same in the for-profit and nonprofit worlds. Consider the situation of the outgoing president of, say, a small college. Staying on the board would provide no monetary compensation and might even entail some monetary penalties (to the extent that there is a heightened expectation of financial contributions from board members, most of whom also pay their own expenses). Staying on the board could entail significant fund-raising responsibilities. And who is to say whether the former president will garner psychic income or feel psychic pain from being reminded regularly of the vicissitudes of fraternity life and the won–lost record of the football team. Nor does the retired head of a nonprofit entity have any need to monitor the value of shares of stock or stock options in "the company." In the nonprofit case, adding up the two sides of the ledger does not suggest that the gains from staying on the board are likely to exceed the costs.

In the corporate world, on the other hand, retired CEOs who continue to serve on boards are compensated for their services in the same manner as are all other nonemployee directors. This usually entails retainers, meeting fees, and eligibility for various benefit programs. In addition, logistical assistance is provided in getting directors to meetings. Thought about purely in terms of tangible rewards, the incentive to remain on the board is surely greater for the corporate CEO than for his counterpart in the nonprofit world. In my view, generous retirement packages should be sufficient recompense for continuing access to the advice and wisdom of a CEO who has retired.

Term Limits and Rotation

8 | Board members should serve defined terms, with upper limits on consecutive years of service; mechanisms should exist for monitoring the performance of board members and assuring turnover.

A recurring problem for corporate boards and nonprofit boards alike is how to replace directors who are not performing up to standard or who simply have served too long. I favor the following:

- Defined regular terms longer than one year.
- Periodic reviews of the performance of directors.
- Overall term limits, as well as mandatory retirement.

Defined Terms of Service

Regular terms longer than the nominal one-year term (which usually guarantees annual reelection) are useful for several reasons. First, it takes time to get to know any organization, and multiyear terms reflect both that reality and the need for directors to make a genuine commitment. Also, the expiration of a real term *can* be used to focus attention on performance.* I underscore the word

---

*In the case of corporate boards, multiyear terms (staggered terms) are also adopted for other reasons, usually as takeover defenses. Institutional shareholders frequently oppose such arrangements precisely because they want to be able to replace an entire board promptly, or to threaten to do so. Nonetheless, I believe that a sensible system of multiyear terms can improve board performance without preventing the proper exercise of shareholder authority.

"can" because it is so difficult under any circumstances to make distinctions among board members, asking some to leave and others to stay.

Performance Reviews

At the minimum, members who fail to meet a reasonable (or even a stiff) attendance requirement should not be renominated, except in the most unusual circumstances. The Securities and Exchange Commission requires corporations to publish the names of directors who attended less than 75 percent of all meetings of the board and of relevant committees, and there is a case to be made for a comparable policy in at least some parts of the nonprofit sector. I have in mind service-providing entities such as Empire Blue Cross and Blue Shield and "stewardship" entities such as United Way. In both of these cases, it would have been useful to know how faithfully board members attended meetings prior to the widely publicized difficulties of their organizations. An even more important question is how many really did their homework, though this is obviously far harder to determine.

I was tempted at one point to suggest a similar policy regarding attendance for all nonprofits, but I am now persuaded that this would be counterproductive. Many grant-seeking nonprofits benefit enormously from the generosity and visible support of key trustees who do not attend many formal meetings of the board. Such arrangements can work, and do work, *provided:* (1) There are effective mechanisms in place for other trustees, perhaps those serving on an executive committee, to provide real oversight and (2) those trustees who are serving de facto as honorary trustees not meddle in operational affairs without spending the time needed to understand the issues. As a practical matter, it would be unwise, in my judgment, to embarrass useful "honorary" board members by emphasizing their nonattendance and perhaps causing them to resign—or, conceivably even worse, causing them to come to more meetings. Principles requiring full participation in board meetings by every trustee are attractive in the abstract, but not always serviceable.

It almost goes without saying that trustees who neither come to meetings nor make other significant contributions should be replaced. The qualifier "almost" is needed because in too many situations, some combination of a sense of courtesy and laziness stands in the way of remedial action. One approach is to encourage individual board members to conduct "self-reviews," asking themselves whether renomination is appropriate. I am told by experienced board members that surprisingly good results can be achieved by well-phrased letters and skillfully handled conversations.

In considering the renomination of directors, some boards focus on changes in an individual's circumstances. Where a significant change occurs (e.g., the person shifts jobs, makes a major geographic move—or is indicted!), the individual can be expected to submit a pro forma resignation that the board's nominating committee then considers. However, it is my impression that this principle is rarely applied effectively.

The importance of collegiality makes it harder, though not impossible, to impose a more stringent standard related directly to substantive aspects of performance. Does the individual think hard about the issues, contribute ideas, and share in the collective responsibility for making decisions? Is the board better off with this individual on the board than it would be if it were to make another appointment? I sense some movement in the direction of a greater willingness to apply more stringent standards—in both the nonprofit and for-profit sectors. The Dow Chemical Company, for example, is experimenting with a formal process whereby individual directors review each other's performance on an anonymous basis. The results are then given to the Board's Committee on Directors, and either the chairman or another member provides counsel as needed. Still, it would be hard to argue that any set of boards has done very well in addressing this problem. One commentator (speaking of corporate boards) was unusually blunt: "It is shameful that boards do not review the performance of their directors and get rid of those who need to be replaced."

Facilitating Turnover: Term Limits and Mandatory Retirement

The most obvious cost of allowing board members to continue serving even if they are not performing well is that they occupy places that could be filled to greater advantage by others. Also, in some situations, board members who fail to understand issues, or to make their points succinctly, can divert and distract the board. In addition, failure to find some effective mechanism for assuring turnover interacts with, and contributes to, the problem of the overly large board discussed earlier. The chairman of one nonprofit board with more than 50 members, who agreed that his board was too large, explained that it has been adding members nonetheless because of a pressing need for new people who could raise money. Because of the lack of an understood way of removing members who had served long enough, this board was—and is—paying a greater price to add new members than it should have to pay.

The achievement of reasonable turnover is also needed to prevent a board from becoming too "tired" and "too set in its ways." The presence of a large number of long-term members who approved setting an organization on a certain course can inhibit looking freshly at established directions and practices.

Mandatory retirement at a specified age is the traditional way of dealing with this class of problems, but it is unlikely to be sufficient, in and of itself. In my view, the best approach is to combine periodic reviews of performance with explicit term limits, carefully constructed to provide the board with a balance between continuity and turnover.

Term limits are particularly effective, in my experience, when they state that no individual who has served successive terms that, in their totality, represent, say, 12 to 15 years of service, can be renominated *without first spending one or two years off the board*. It is then much easier to reelect a particularly valuable member without grossly offending that individual's "classmates" (who at least will be absent when the discussion and vote occur). This presumes that reelection of those members who have sat out will not become normal practice, which would obviate the purpose of the limit. Similarly, while bylaws can be set aside when special situations present themselves, it is important that this practice not become routine.

Term limits are likely to be the most effective way of dealing with board members who are adequate but not exceptional contributors. While some worry that term limits will also cause outstanding individuals to be lost to the board, this has not been my experience. Those who are strongly committed to an institution will understand the need for such a mechanism. Term limits also make it easier to select relatively young members, since there is no risk that someone will serve uninterruptedly for as long as three decades or more.

An early advocate of term limits, Ken Dayton, in a speech given eight years ago, observed:

> Frankly it seems to me that in some respects the independent sector is ahead of the corporate sector in regard to board policies on balance and rotation. . . . When we instituted a 12-year rotation policy for outside Dayton-Hudson directors, we could find no other American Corporation with a similar policy. Yet many Independent Sector members have even more stringent policies. . . .[12]

The greater historic appeal of term limits to nonprofits may be due to the typically larger sizes of their boards. In any case, the interest in term limits has increased in the corporate world since Dayton's talk. The most recent Korn/Ferry survey reports: "Forty-two percent of the respondents believe there should be a limit to a director's term of service; up from 29 percent in 1990. Those who favor a limit believe it should be 12 years."[13]

It is not hard to think of examples of long-term directors who have been invaluable in bringing about needed change, and there is a risk that rigid rules will deprive a board of the services of those who have thought longest about the organization and may even be the most willing to go out on the proverbial limb. But a modicum of flexibility, combined with skillful management of the processes of rotation and reelection, should make it possible to retain the advantages of continuity without subjecting the board and the organization to overly long service by those who should have retired years ago.

One other comment: While mechanical mechanisms for dealing with board rotation are fine, and will help, there is simply no substitute for what Bruce Atwater calls "the will to act." Assessing the performance of board members up for reelection should be a principal responsibility of an independent nominating committee and its chairman, as I shall emphasize in Chapter 4. No set of rules or presumptions can solve this set of problems absent determination to do the right thing.

"Doing the right thing" does not include using a vigorous process of evaluation to weed out idiosyncratic directors who are viewed by some as "troublemakers." That would be an abuse of discretion that could have a chilling effect. A more radical solution to the whole problem of board rotation would be to appoint board members to a single, fixed term (say 7–10 years), with no possibility of reelection. One commentator who favors this approach says it would be ". . . a sort of modified Federal Reserve Board rule. With careful selection, it removes any possible inhibitions to show courage and follow one's conscience. Probably not doable, but worthwhile to consider."

Optimist that I am, I do not think that such a fail-safe mechanism is needed to protect the essential freedom to speak out. Perversion of the evaluation process to discipline constructive dissidents would not be tolerated by any board that is serious about achieving its purposes. And no contrarian is likely to be of much use, in any case, on a board that would operate in such a fashion.

Compensation of Directors

Board compensation is an aspect of governance that lends itself to more precise rule making. Finding the right rules can be complicated, however. Presumptions should differ, not only between the for-profit and nonprofit sectors broadly defined, but also within the nonprofit sector.

9 | **Compensation of directors of for-profit corporations should be reasonable, and board members should receive no additional compensation beyond that provided for service on the board itself: There should be no additional consulting fees or other special benefits.**

In the case of corporate boards, payment should adequately reflect the responsibilities involved in serving as a director and should be high enough to attract requisite talent. But care should be taken to avoid paying so much that directors are tempted to "hold their fire," lest they jeopardize their positions as directors by offending the CEO or other powerful board members. Michael Blumenthal once referred to those who come to meetings simply to collect their fees as "rice-bowl directors."

I certainly recognize the force of Blumenthal's point, which I fear applies in more instances than most of us would like to acknowledge. But I doubt that much, if anything, would be accomplished by pushing for large reductions in current levels of compensation. (The continuing debate over high levels of executive compensation is much more significant, and also much more intense.)

Remuneration seems to be less of a problem in inhibiting independence on corporate boards than other factors. Moreover, proposals to reduce compensation risk discouraging participation by individuals who come from noncorporate occupations. Richard Lyman offered the following candid comment on an earlier draft:

> I confess to having winced a little at the point about not making Directors' pay large enough to inhibit their feeling free to jeopardize their positions by speaking up. Few directors of major corporations are in such modest circumstances that their compensation as directors matters a whole lot to them, but I've been one such. If it is thought desirable to have noncorporate types on corporate boards . . . this problem will crop up now and then. For the rest, however, I think corporate groupthink and the club atmosphere among fellow-CEOs are far more of a problem in causing directors to "hold their fire" than fear of losing income.

A number of thoughtful people have argued that compensation for service on corporate boards, far from being too high, is too low to recognize adequately the time commitment required and the liabilities accepted.[14] While this may be true in some situations, I am not persuaded by this general line of argument either. I support another approach, which might either lower or raise overall compensation depending on outcomes; namely, a higher share of the remuneration of corporate board members should be put "at risk," perhaps through greater use of stock options. This is also the approach that I think should be taken in setting executive compensation.

A related question concerns compensation provided to directors who simultaneously serve the company in other capacities, usually as consultants. I can state my own view succinctly: *Individuals should be either board members or consultants, never both at the same time.* Otherwise, directors who also serve as consultants may feel some loyalty to those who engaged them (usually the CEO), when they must be loyal only to the shareholders who elected them. Divided allegiances—or even perceptions of divided allegiances—can create serious problems, especially when the board evaluates the performance of the CEO.

10 | Directors of certain classes of nonprofits (those that provide services but do not seek contributions) should also be compensated; but directors of "charitable" nonprofits, which seek contributions from others, should contribute their own services.

The issue of compensation for trustees of nonprofit entities is, surprisingly, more complex. My own view, perhaps iconoclastic, is that the generic problem in this sector may be the opposite of the one faced by for-profit boards: too little tangible reward in certain circumstances rather than too rich a gruel. While there are occasional outrages, the most common pattern is for directors of nonprofit entities to serve without any compensation at all. We should think hard about the wisdom of this convention, and whether it continues to make sense in all contexts. Confronting the compensation question directly has the virtue of raising the most fundamental issues concerning service on nonprofit boards—why individuals serve and what responsibilities go with board membership.

My view is that we need to distinguish rather sharply between two polar sets of nonprofits: (1) providers of services, such as Empire Blue Cross and Blue Shield, which do not seek contributions and (2) the so-called charitable nonprofits, such as universities, orchestras, and museums, which depend heavily on the generosity of donors. I believe that the directors of the first class of nonprofits should be compensated, but that the directors (or trustees) of the charitable nonprofits should contribute their services. Private foundations constitute a third, intermediate class of organizations, which in these respects often resemble the category (1) institutions more than they do the grant-seekers in category (2). Thus it is not surprising that foundations, especially the large foundations, typically compensate their directors.

The main reason I favor compensating the directors of service-providing nonprofits is that the lack of compensation can encourage the feeling that whatever they do or don't do is fine, since, after all, they are "only volunteers."[15] Paying directors of this class of nonprofit organizations at least a nominal fee would make it clear that significant services are to be rendered; interestingly, the newly appointed chairman of Empire has made precisely this recommendation. In its lead editorial describing this proposal, titled "The Sound of Snoring at Empire," the *New York Times* commented: "The pay wouldn't cost very much and would send a signal heard by members of other corporate boards: You're hired to do an important job, so get to work."[16]

Compensating directors of nonprofit entities such as Empire Blue Cross makes sense for a related reason. Legal accountability depends on the presence of compensation:

> Section 720-a of New York's Not-for-Profit Corporation Law causes compensated directors of New York not-for-profits to be held to a higher standard of accountability than their uncompensated counterparts (or perhaps more correctly lowers the standard to which uncompensated directors are held).[17]

Providing direct compensation may also discourage the substitution of other, less visible, "perks." In the Empire Blue Cross case, government investigators have unearthed evidence of lavish gifts purchased for directors (ornate silver punch bowls, cashmere blankets, etc.). Apparently the corresponding Maryland plan paid $300,000 for a sky box at Oriole Park in Baltimore, and an executive of the Washington plan is said "to have traveled to Bermuda, Portugal, and Switzerland to see whether certain resorts were appropriate for Blue Cross meetings."[18] As a de facto matter, "compensation" surely was provided to these nonprofit directors, and it would have been better, in my view, if the arrangements had been more direct and more visible. The entire Empire Blue Cross experience also raises the much more complex question of how such organizations should be set up and supervised in the first place. It is by no means clear that traditional nonprofit status is appropriate.

Why don't the same arguments apply to compensation for directors of all nonprofits, including those that depend on contributed income? In principle, they do. But there are also offsetting considerations, which seem more powerful.

First, providing even token compensation to trustees of this second set of nonprofit boards could have the perverse effect of reducing their sense of financial obligation—their generosity—to the organizations they serve. While it is possible for directors of grant-seeking nonprofits to give back any nominal fees that they are paid, just as they normally make other contributions, it is hard to know how many would elect this option. Moreover, some trustees might feel that by returning their fee they had done all that they should be expected to do; that is, the existence of an opportunity to give back modest fees might actually make it harder to extract meaningful contributions from all board members.

The perilous financial state of many nonprofit entities also argues against compensating their directors. As Taylor Reveley observes:

> When there's not enough money to pay the staff a living wage, or to have decent office space and equipment, or to keep creditors easily at bay . . . , it would be hard to explain even trifling fees for trustees.

The argument of principle is finally the most powerful of all. Robert Goheen echoes the views of many:

> I frankly do not like the notion of pay for trustees of nonprofit institutions like universities, museums, and research organizations. In my view trustees should serve because they believe in what the institution is doing (or trying to do) and want to help it do it well (or better). If they don't have that commitment, I doubt a modest fee will make them more zealous. . . . Trustees of course should be assured that *all* expenses connected with Board-related service will be covered by the institution.

The combined force of all these points explains why board compensation is so uncommon among charitable nonprofits—and why, in my view, it would be unwise to alter the present convention.

4

How Boards Are Organized

The norms in this chapter all pertain to the internal workings of boards and are related in one way or another to the pivotal relationship between the CEO and the board. Graef Crystal titled his book on executive compensation *In Search of Excess.*[1] A comparable title for this chapter might be "In Search of Balance," since a principal theme is the importance of achieving a better balance between the need for focused executive direction of organizations and the need for effective oversight by boards of directors. The chapter begins with an extended discussion of the complex and contentious issue of whether the CEO should also chair the board and then turns to committee structures, the conduct of board meetings, the role of outside advisors, and management succession.

The Pros and Cons of a Nonexecutive Chairman or "Lead Director"

11 | **The board should have either a nonexecutive chairman or an alternative structure (such as a strong committee on the board led by an outside director) that will allow the board to discharge its obligations without usurping managerial functions.**

This norm reflects common practice in the nonprofit world, though certainly not in the corporate world. I believe that it has merit in both settings.

In the nonprofit world, it is rare for the CEO to chair the board. Most commonly, there is a division of labor, with a paid executive (often called the president or executive director) functioning as CEO alongside a part-time, usually unpaid, chairman, who is the leading lay trustee. An informal study of nonprofit organizations receiving grants from the Mellon Foundation (conducted by Margaret McKenna) revealed that the CEO was also the chairman in less than 10 percent of the cases. Most of the exceptions were foreign organizations, entities still led by their founders, or literary presses that may have evolved only recently from for-profit status.

While nonprofit boards have numerous shortcomings, this is one respect in which customary arrangements seem to work reasonably well and to be generally accepted. Accordingly, I shall focus most of the ensuing discussion on corporate boards, coming back only at the end of the chapter to the intriguing question of why established patterns are so different in the two sectors.*

---

*Ironically, the contentious issue in the nonprofit world is not whether the CEO should chair the board, but whether the CEO should even be a voting member. At a recent meeting in Washington, D.C., sponsored by the National Center for Nonprofit Boards ("Accountability at the Crossroads," November 14–16, 1993), this was a major subject of debate. According to one line of argument, voting membership would constitute a conflict of interest; the other side argued that voting membership was symbolic evidence of the CEO's position. My own view is that the CEO should definitely be a voting member of the board, primarily to indicate that the CEO should be regarded as a peer of the other trustees, not merely as a hired hand. It is impossible even to imagine a similar debate in a corporate context, which is simply another way of noting the extent of the difference between the two sectors in their assumptions about the right relationship between the CEO and the board.

The Case for a Nonexecutive Chairman

There has been a great deal of debate about the desirability of separating the roles of CEO and chairman in for-profit corporations. Much of it stems from dissatisfaction with what has seemed to many to be an excessive concentration of power in the hands of a single person. In John Whitehead's words:

> One-man rule is a bad idea. A single CEO-chairman can do great damage before being reined in—often when it is too late, or almost too late.

Within the past few years, several well-known corporations (General Motors, American Express, and Westinghouse) elected separate chairmen who were not themselves former CEOs of the company.* While these may all prove to have been transitory arrangements, they illustrate the attention being paid to the recurring question of what constitutes the best governing structure for corporate boards.[2]

One of the strongest statements on this subject was made by Kenneth Dayton in 1985:

> All my experience and study have convinced me that the chairman of the board should not be the CEO—not in an American public corporation and certainly not in a philanthropic institution. Why? . . . A chairman/CEO wears two hats at the same time and you just can't do that and look good in both roles. . . . He/she is in a delicate

---

*In what follows, whenever I speak of a "nonexecutive chairman" or a "separate chairman," I mean someone who was not previously the CEO of the same company. Electing an outside director as chairman is very different from asking the previous CEO to continue as chairman, and the two models must be distinguished. Unfortunately, this is rarely done. For example, the Korn/Ferry surveys of the frequency of nonexecutive chairmen lump both categories together.

position between the CEO and the board, letting the
CEO make necessary reports and recommendations,
supporting the CEO, and sometimes even protecting the
CEO. But at the same time, he/she must make certain that
suggestions, challenges, even criticisms are heard and
considered. In my view no one can do all that and be
the CEO as well. I know; I tried it. If the chairman is
also the CEO, he/she makes the agenda, conducts
the meeting, presents management's recommendations,
controls the discussion, and asks for support of his/her
own recommendations. When one does all that and in
addition usually picks his/her fellow board members, you
have in my opinion a dictatorship. It may be benign and it
may even be enlightened, but it is nonetheless a
dictatorship. In my view, any chairman/CEO inevitably
wears primarily his/her CEO hat and only occasionally
takes on the far more neutral and impartial role of the
chairman of the board.[3]

Jay Lorsch, in his empirical study of the powers of the corporate
CEO who also chairs the board, has stressed not just the formal levers
of control, including control over the flow of information, but also
what he calls "unspoken norms [that] dictate the actual course of
behavior in the boardroom:"

Directors are expected, above all, to treat the CEO with
respect, which means not embarrassing him or her in a
board meeting. . . . Since directors shouldn't openly
criticize the CEO, the accepted way of objecting is to ask
penetrating questions.
    Also de rigueur is not contacting fellow directors out
of meetings. One director [interviewed for Lorsch's study]
explained: "That's taboo. We feel that would be dealing
behind the chairman's back."

Lorsch concludes:

> The reluctance to violate group norms and the practical obstacles to unity may not create problems in healthy companies, but . . . they can delay the recognition of emerging problems and create serious difficulties for boards dealing with crises.[4]

I agree with the thrust of these arguments. But I also want to emphasize that combining the roles of CEO and chairman in one person, as is usually done, can work well. I have served on several corporate boards in which CEO-chairmen have performed superbly in both roles, and I know that many other directors could provide similar testimony.

To be sure, these have tended to be successful companies on a proverbial "roll." Still, in at least one situation of which I have personal knowledge (when NCR was being taken over by AT&T), life was far from calm, and the CEO-chairman, Charles Exley, was nothing less than masterful in his struggles on behalf of the NCR shareholders. But even in this instance, when the CEO had a well-deserved reputation for competence and integrity (and also owned a large number of shares personally), there were snide comments by institutional investors suggesting that he might be putting the interests of management ahead of the interests of shareholders. A supportive, nonexecutive chairman might have helped somewhat with the issue of appearances, even though it would have been impossible, in my judgment, to have improved on Exley's results. Also, we need to recognize that NCR's shareholders might not have been blessed with a CEO who identified so strongly with their interests.*

---

*The ironies in deciding who really represents shareholder interests are illustrated well by stories Exley told about this experience in his lecture in the Manhattan College John J. Horan Lecture Series (Vol. 2, pp. 15–16). While Exley himself had tens of millions of dollars of his own at risk, he nonetheless found himself challenged by representatives of institutional shareholders who had, as he put it, "not a nickel of their own money at stake." Even more interesting is the conundrum presented by massive index funds. Here is Exley's account of one

The point, then, is not that combining these roles can never work—a proposition at variance with reality. The model of a single CEO-chairman does, however, deprive the board of an important protection against abuses of power. It decreases the likelihood that the CEO (and all board members, for that matter) will hear the kinds of authentic "second opinions" that should be expressed by a truly independent board. Provision for a separate chairman also underscores the point that the CEO reports to the board, not the other way around. In practical terms, the presence of a non-CEO chairman provides a structure whereby the board itself has a clearly understood role in nominating board members, appointing board committees, setting agendas and, if need be, selecting independent advisors to the board. These seemingly innocent-sounding powers (discussed further in the following sections) can be very important. Finally, the presence of a separate chairman facilitates the regular review of the performance of the CEO and avoids any risk that a CEO might preside at a discussion of his own future.

An argument from experience in favor of the separate chairman model is that it has worked well, over many years, in a wide variety of nonprofit institutions, some of which are quite complex. Though rarely cited, this is relevant evidence. Also, I am told that this model has been used successfully by corporations in Australia and in Europe, and by U.S. companies at various times, especially prior to World War II.

---

such situation: "At one index fund, their position was explained to me this way: 'Mr. Exley, we are against this takeover and think it would be a bad thing for both companies. However, we are told by AT&T that this takeover is inevitable. We have 18 times the investment in AT&T that we have in NCR. That being the case, we think it is in our interest to have the deal completed at the lowest possible cost to AT&T. . . .' I felt that I had stepped through the looking glass. I wondered what the other NCR holders would think of this exercise of shareholder rights."

So far as I am aware, this phenomenon has not been addressed by the SEC. As one person who heard this story commented: "What we have here is a walking conflict of interest."

Arguments Against

Persuaded as I am of its intrinsic appeal, I am convinced that the notion of a separate chairman on corporate boards is not an idea whose time has come. I say this in spite of having received a significant number of endorsements of the concept by commentators who are highly regarded business leaders, including one former CEO who had previously opposed the idea. We should not minimize the degree to which this concept has taken hold. The overwhelming majority of CEOs, however, remain strongly opposed—which is hardly surprising.[5]

Another empirical reality is that in almost all cases in which companies have elected separate chairmen, they have done so only for a transitional period, usually in the aftermath of upheavals. American Express and Westinghouse have now recombined the positions of chairman and CEO. General Motors still has a separate chairman, but this is, as far as I am aware, the only extant large-company case of its kind.[6]

It is surprisingly difficult to find a cogent summary of the reasons so many experienced people have come down against the concept of a separate chairman. The fullest statement I have been able to locate is, ironically, by proponents of the basic idea, Martin Lipton and Jay Lorsch:

> The principal arguments against such separation are that: (a) it would dilute the power of the CEO to provide effective leadership of the company, (b) it creates the potential for rivalry between the chairperson and the CEO, leading to compromise rather than crisp decisiveness, (c) the chairperson may be overly protective of the CEO and shield the CEO from being held accountable by the board for poor performance, and (d) having two public spokespersons leads to confusion and the opportunity for third parties to take advantage of the division.[7]

The danger of a board chairman acting like management is probably greatest in the nonprofit sector. In one part of his speech on governance, Ken Dayton remarked: "I regret to tell you that I have known volunteer chairmen of the [nonprofit] board who clearly think that they are the CEO. And, even more I regret to tell you, I have known paid executives who ought to be the CEO but who are not, and who are perfectly willing to let the board and/or its chairman call the shots."[8] The solution to problems of this kind, if one exists, resides in recruitment of stronger executive leadership and the election of better-disciplined boards. Also relevant, I suspect, is the sometime-tendency for boards of nonprofits to believe they are accountable only to themselves.

Whatever reservations we may have about some of the arguments against having a separate chairman (viewed either on their own terms or compared with the opposing arguments), the very fact that they are held strongly by respected CEOs must be taken into account. As a practical matter, a board of a for-profit company is unlikely to do battle with an effective CEO over such an issue. Whatever the abstract merits, as long as the concept of a separate chairman is so rarely embraced by the corporate world, it will inevitably have more than a slight hint of the unseemly about it. CEOs asked to accept such an arrangement will wonder if a non-CEO chairmanship implies lack of confidence in them. ("*Real* leaders are chairmen as well as CEOs, so why not me?") It is ludicrous to imagine IBM contemplating for even one moment the recruitment of a nationally respected CEO of Louis Gerstner's stature without simultaneously offering him the chairmanship.

It is impossible to know if resistance to the idea of a separate chairman will diminish over time. For my own part, I hope that at least some other companies follow the lead of GM and try out the idea, so that it can be tested more thoroughly in the corporate context. The best opportunities to move in this direction are likely to occur when a CEO-chairman steps down and an internal candidate is chosen as the next CEO; in at least some situations (especially when the newly elected CEO is fairly young), it may be feasible to name an outside director chairman and then see how the arrangement works. In any event, under the best of circumstances it will take considerable time for a distinctively new model to evolve, if it ever does.

Meanwhile, the wise course is surely to see if there are less contentious, and less disruptive, ways of achieving the core objectives. I believe that there are. Bestowing the title of chairman on an outside director is by no means the only approach. My own view is that the best first step that can be taken now is for boards to establish a strong "committee on the board" (or "committee on governance"), to be chaired by an outside director and to be given a number of the key responsibilities that might otherwise be entrusted to a separate chairman. But before examining this specific proposal in more detail, we should consider the more general concept of a lead director.

The "Lead Director" Approach

This is the alternative favored by a number of people, including Lipton and Lorsch, who appear to have backed away from the idea of a separate chairman for the practical reasons already stated: There is just too much opposition to it. In making the case for a lead director, they write: "What this person is called is not important, but his or her duties are important."[9]

I agree that the definition of duties matters most, but phraseology and the title chosen are also important—more important than Lipton and Lorsch believe them to be. The phrase "lead director" is itself capable of arousing strong emotions; it detracts from the objectives being sought. Some other directors (perhaps perceiving themselves as consigned to rank-and-file status) may resent the notion that any other outside director is to be so designated. They may insist that every member has equal obligations under the law, which is surely true.

They may also believe that there is no need for such a supernumerary.

It is instructive to consider a specific example of how the general concept has been applied, setting aside for the moment the phrase lead director itself. To cite a case from the nonprofit sector with which I am familiar, at Princeton no one had the title of chairman of the board (an unusual arrangement, to be sure); the president presided at board meetings. However, there was an outside chairman of the executive committee, who participated in setting the agenda for board meetings, who took the vote when the president made recommendations requiring board action, who was responsible for organizing evaluations of the president's performance, who took main responsibility for the organization of the board itself, including the nomination of new trustees and of committee chairmen, and so on. (The "and so on" was defined broadly to include marching at the head of the traditional procession of classes, the "P-Rade," at Reunions!) The identity of the lead trustee was known to everyone, and the system has worked well for many years, with different individuals in the key positions.

In that setting, the outside chairman of the executive committee also performed a number of other useful functions. A good description of the informal aspects of the role has been provided by John C. Kenefick, former chairman of the Union Pacific Railroad and a person who functioned very effectively in this capacity:

> To work at all, of course, the "lead director" must be formally recognized with some sort of title; and he must be prepared to give the job some time so that he will know generally what is going on, but without intruding in or interfering with the responsibilities of the chief executive officer. In any event, in addition to the obvious functions, I believe he and only he can play certain very important roles:

First, act as an intermediary between the outside directors and the CEO. On occasion an outside director will be reluctant to ask what might be a sensitive question publicly but can be comfortable asking that question of the lead director, who is a colleague. The lead director can answer the question himself or get an answer. He can pass on to the CEO ideas or opinions which come to him from individual outside directors and also, of course, do the reverse: explain to individual directors the policies of the administration.

Second, detect possible problems early on, consult with the CEO and, when appropriate, discreetly warn outside directors. He can offer a comfort factor to his colleagues who know someone on their side is watching the shop.

Finally, if worst comes to worst and it appears a change of CEO must be made, provide the mechanism, first to evaluate the situation and then, if necessary, to make the change in a timely and efficient way.

It is a delicate role, but it can work.

The extent to which particular functions need to be performed will vary from situation to situation and from time to time. The size of the board and the number of new members, for instance, will affect the importance of the intermediary role. Where boards are small and members are experienced, there may be little need for that function in normal times: Board members will have no hesitation in going directly to the CEO with questions, comments, and suggestions.

Still, even if it is rarely used, there is much to be said for having an authorized place within the organizational structure to which directors can go to register concerns and check impressions, especially when an organization seems to be in trouble or to be missing opportunities. The alternatives are not good ones: suppressed concerns, sub rosa grumbling, or the formation of informal "cabals" outside the regular channels. As I can attest from painful experience, the unstructured, informal approach can entail high costs. In addition to irritating people and encouraging splits in a board, it also operates slowly and is dependent on the more or less accidental emergence of a director prepared to take the lead. Counting on some spontaneously generated process to solve major problems is not sensible, and one commentator (Arjay Miller) surely spoke for others in arguing strongly against relying on ad hoc machinery. A board should be prepared to cope with the most important problems that could arise, such as the need to replace the CEO before he is prepared to step down, while hoping always that such preparation will prove unnecessary.

A major responsibility, then, of a lead director is to function on standby, to serve as an insurance policy on which the board prefers never to collect. A great virtue of this particular "policy" is that it is cheap—precisely because such a person may also be helpful in normal times and may, in fact, assist in preventing the most serious kinds of crises from ever reaching a boiling point.

Brief mention should be made of another potentially important function that can be served by a lead director in a corporate context. Such a person can be a point of contact with large institutional investors, giving them, as outsiders, another recognized place to go to raise questions and voice concerns. In the case of American Express, Richard Furlaud (first as separate chairman and subsequently as chairman of the executive committee) has functioned very effectively in this capacity.

In certain contexts, the presence of a lead director or separate chairman can also serve to protect both the CEO and the board in general from what Alan Pifer refers to as "the occasional bully who can appear on any board." Controlling such behavior is necessary, especially on nonprofit boards, if staff members are not to be intimidated. While (mercifully) I have been spared this class of problems and have no personal experiences to recount, chilling testimonials by Pifer and others leave no doubt that efforts by domineering board members to dictate to staff can be extremely dangerous. A strong chairman or lead director may be more effective than a CEO in curbing such tendencies and, if necessary, in seeking the resignation of the offender. The CEO, after all, reports to the board—and therefore to any bullies who may be on it.

Serving all these functions obviously requires judgment and tact. The lead director must be careful not to suggest, by word or deed, that he is competing with the CEO for authority, and he must not second-guess the CEO; he must also make clear that he does not function in a managerial role and is not authorized to make decisions. The CEO and the lead director need to work closely and comfortably together, as they generally do in the nonprofit world. They need to help each other, respecting their complementary roles.

An obvious risk is that the wrong person might be chosen as lead director. Great care needs to be exercised in the selection, with all board members, as well as the CEO, being consulted individually. In addition, there should be an explicit understanding that there will be turnover in the position. Ideally, other well-qualified directors will be chairing major committees, and they provide another kind of balance in the organizational structure.

One CEO (Frank Popoff of Dow Chemical) has said that, in his view, there should be "many lead directors," each responsible for a defined territory. There is much to be said for this idea, especially since it also reduces the risk that the CEO and "the" lead director will become, as another person put it, "too cozy." Establishing multiple points of authority makes good sense, *provided* that key functions, centered on the effective functioning of the board itself, are understood to be the primary responsibility of one person—or, as suggested in the next section, of one committee.

A Committee on the Board

In thinking about practical steps to achieve some of these objectives, my own preference is to avoid the term "lead director" and instead to focus specifically on the need to have directors other than the CEO exercise primary responsibility for the effective functioning of the board itself. A simple approach is to establish an influential board committee on governance (which could be called that, or called simply "the committee on the board"), with a senior outside director serving as chairman and membership limited to outside directors. The CEO would meet with the committee as appropriate but would not be a member. A committee of this kind could replace the usual kind of nominating committee and assume its duties: nominating new directors, reviewing the performance of current directors, and nominating individuals to chair standing committees. It could also take special responsibility for evaluating and seeking to improve board processes, including the setting of agendas, the conduct of board meetings, and the flow of information to directors.

In addition, I believe that the committee on the board (and certainly its chairman) should play an important role in guiding the board's evaluation of the CEO. While this aspect of the governance committee's work has to be coordinated with the activities of the compensation committee, there is much to be said for distinguishing the responsibility of the board for evaluating the performance of the CEO from its responsibility for reviewing the recommendations of the CEO concerning the compensation of other officers of the company, who report to the CEO. These are basically different functions.

The chairman of my proposed committee on the board could also serve such other functions as stipulated by his colleagues, including some of those associated with the idea of a lead director. But the central mission of the committee and its chairman would be defined and limited: to focus on the effective operation of the board itself—on its membership, its structure, and its work habits. While nominating committees serve some of these functions, they do not serve all of them, and they generally lack the status and focus that seem to me important.

This approach has the advantage of locating core responsibilities for governance in a specified place while preserving the collective character of board governance. The chairman of the committee on the board would obviously be important, but he would still only be the chairman and would have to work with the other members of the committee. The committee itself would report to the board as a whole and one of its important responsibilities would be to see that no director felt excluded from discussions of these important matters. Other committees, including the executive committee, would continue to discharge their own duties, and there would be no suggestion that this committee occupied a superior place in the organizational hierarchy.

In short, the establishment of a committee on the board need not be as unsettling as the appointment of a separate chairman or lead director. It would surely not appear to be as revolutionary a step. But it could prove to be a deceptively powerful, and useful, instrument of effective governance.

In concluding this discussion, I want to underscore a central point made by Ron Daniel: Progress in adopting and following most of the other norms and "structural propositions" that I advance depends on, in his words, "working through this vexing issue." And, as Daniel and others have emphasized, it will not be easy for corporations to embrace this norm—to find acceptable ways of giving outside directors effective control of board governance—even if it is thought, in the abstract, to make sense.

Habit and inertia are powerful forces, especially when organizations are doing just fine as is. So long as earnings are reasonably good, executive compensation does not appear utterly inappropriate, and all other vital signs are positive, it is unlikely that shareholders will exert strong pressure for new modes of governance. Major changes in board organization are most likely to occur in the wake of difficulties and dramatic developments, such as the removal of a CEO or the restructuring of a company. Even then, as we have seen, such changes are often hard to sustain.

At the same time, if there can be a greater willingness on the part of some corporations to experiment with variants of the concepts outlined here, a number of others might then move in similar directions. Progress in such matters is almost always episodic and tends to be based on emulation of existing models. What is needed is a larger number of examples in the for-profit sector for others to consider. In this regard, it may be significant that IBM recently established a committee on "directors and corporate governance" that appears to have most of the features I have just outlined.[10] Colleagues on the board of American Express are discussing similar ideas.

We should also encourage experiments with more radical approaches, such as the appointment of a separate chairman. More evidence from the for-profit sector would then be available to complement that derived from the extensive experiences of nonprofit institutions with separate chairmen, lead directors, and related committee structures. We must not forget, however, that there are profound differences between the two sectors in their traditional approaches to this key organizational issue and that the reasons for these deeply rooted differences may argue for the continuing desirability of separate models. The last part of this chapter explores these divergent histories.

Committee Structures

12 | **Committees should not make major policy decisions for the board as a whole.**

As the previous discussion illustrates, the structure and functioning of the committees established by a board are extremely important. The use made of committees in a particular institutional setting naturally depends greatly on the size of the board. Large boards have no option but to conduct much of their business through committees, while small boards can function more as "committees of the whole."

Whatever the size and structure, a cardinal principle is that committees should report to the board as a whole and should not abrogate to themselves decision-making power. Exceptions to this generalization include the need for executive committees to act between meetings of the board and for specialized committees, such as investment committees, to act on detailed matters that fall within the area of authority delegated to them by the board. Even in these cases, however, all members of the board should be kept fully informed of the activities of the committees and included in policy discussions.

This norm is most frequently violated, I suspect, by large nonprofit boards facing hard choices. At Wilson College, in Chambersburg, Pennsylvania (a small liberal arts college for women that nearly closed in the early 1970s), members of the minority on the board who opposed the original decision to close the college criticized the practice of allowing a small group of trustees, functioning as an executive committee and acting in concert with the president, to make decisions without any real discussion within the board as a whole. Opponents of closure claimed that the board was given no real option but to ratify what the president and the committee had done already.[11]

In the equally contentious saga of the University of Bridgeport, which was ultimately "rescued," "bailed out," or "acquired" (depending on the connotation preferred) by a group funded by Sun Myung Moon and his followers, it has been alleged that key decisions to borrow large sums of money were made by the Finance and Executive Committees and were ratified later by the board as a whole only when they were in effect irreversible (see Appendix B).

13 | Committee structures should reflect the needs of each organization and should facilitate the exercise of independent judgment by outside directors, including the nomination of new directors.

The existence of various kinds of committees should be expected to vary across institutional types, reflecting the range of purposes served by for-profit and nonprofit organizations. A large museum may well have a committee on the sensitive subject of deaccessioning; and the board of a college with an active alumni group may want to have a committee concerned with alumni relations.

Core Committees

All boards also have common needs. At the minimum, there is a strong argument for having within any board structure audit, compensation and personnel, and nominating committees (or, as I have suggested, a committee on the board in place of a nominating committee), plus an executive committee capable of acting between meetings of the full board. I suspect that these core functions are represented more consistently in the organizational structures of for-profit boards, in part because of legal and regulatory requirements and in part because the voluntary nature of board membership may limit the time that trustees devote to committee work. Whatever the explanation, the committee structures of some nonprofit boards appear to be too casual in this regard.

Independent directors increasingly make up the entire membership of the three core committees, with management and staff preparing materials and, at times, participating in discussions, but not as committee members. Independent directors customarily meet alone, at least for parts of meetings. This too seems generally agreed and appropriate.

The nominating function is often particularly sensitive, as well as obviously important. *The board itself, through its own nominating process, should play the decisive role in the selection of new directors.* Self-evident as this precept may seem, it is by no means always followed in either the nonprofit or for-profit sectors. As many people have testified, domination by the CEO can occur in spite of the existence of an apparently independent nominating committee. The most recent Korn/Ferry survey states:

> Many of the old rules continue to apply. Getting seated on a board still depends, in large part, on who you know. Fully 89 percent of the companies surveyed locate board members through the recommendations of the chairman.[12]

Needless to say, the objective should not be to discourage the CEO from contributing suggestions, but only to be sure that the CEO does not dictate board selection. In the case of both corporate and nonprofit boards, the CEO will often have to play a pivotal role in persuading individuals with many claims on their time to serve. Because close and satisfying working relationships between the CEO and board members are critical to effective governance, the personal involvement of the CEO in recruiting board members is essential. It does not follow, however, that others on the board should be kept from having a real role in the selection process and be left only to "vote right" when a slate is presented.

To be effective, the nominating process must be systematic; too often, it is haphazard. Arjay Miller argues strongly in favor of using professional search firms, on the grounds that they maintain good files, they can identify potential conflicts of interest, and they may even be able to make some initial contacts with less awkwardness than the CEO or another board member. Others may resist this approach, for good reasons or bad ones. Much depends on the quality of both the search firm in question and the internal search process that can be mounted in the absence of outside help. One way or another, boards should work hard at finding the "right" nominees.

The recruitment of directors who are both well qualified and well suited to the work of an organization can be an even more challenging task for nonprofits. Small, relatively unknown entities may have a hard time identifying appropriate candidates. Fortunately, the need for assistance in this area is increasingly recognized. For example, a group in New York, called the Volunteer Consulting Group, was created to serve precisely this function.

Committees of corporate boards charged with nominating new directors need to insist on meeting without the CEO. Many of us have been in situations in which the CEO, while not a member of the nominating committee, meets with it always and guides its deliberations—sometimes with a heavy hand. Directors are not always as willing to challenge the CEO as they should be, and the committee process itself should not make it harder than it needs to be for them to act independently.

14 | The chairman of the compensation committee should be a resolutely independent soul, and no one director should occupy that position for very long.

How committees of all kinds function depends critically on who chairs them. An important advantage of the board committee model described earlier is its provision of a mechanism for discouraging the CEO from playing too dominant a role in making such selections. The separate chairman model has the same advantage.

The choice of the chairman can be decisive in the case of the compensation committee. A commentator observed ruefully that he had served on one board where the chairmanship of the compensation committee was held by the same person for more than a decade, and that this individual behaved in a highly predictable manner:

> His ability to defend sizable increases for the top officers was totally unconnected with how well or how badly the company was doing at any given time. When things went well, the chairman (CEO) had to be rewarded; when disaster struck, his morale had to be protected (dark references to a depressed mood, etc.). . . . I suspect that the norm in the corporate world is for the CEO to

find a chairman of executive compensation who can be counted on to behave this way—and then stick with that choice.

I am less skeptical about standard practice, though evidence is hard to obtain. In most companies, attitudes toward executive compensation seem to be rather different today, with more emphasis given to defining, and sticking with, policies that relate compensation to corporate performance. Recent SEC disclosure requirements are relevant in this regard. The obvious procedural safeguards, in any event, are to be sure that the CEO does not personally choose the chairman of the compensation committee and that the position rotates.

While the compensation committee and the full board have an inescapable responsibility to think carefully about all aspects of executive compensation, including the establishment of incentives that tie the fortunes of the top executives to those of the shareholders, this entire process can become excessively complicated and overly time consuming. Corporate boards and their compensation committees sometimes devote more time and attention to compensation than to more important matters such as the evaluation of strategic directions.

Meeting Formats and Scheduling

15 | Boards should meet with reasonable frequency, and board agendas and board calendars should assure time for discussion of the most important topics.

The number of board meetings per year should depend on the use made of committees and the consequences of waiting on actions by the full board for significant periods of times. The appropriate number might range from, say, four to ten. Meetings should be frequent enough that members do not forget what transpired at the previous meeting. Another reason for frequent, and more than perfunctory, meetings is that members need to get to know each other well enough to work cohesively under pressure, should that become necessary. It is hard to imagine an effective board meeting fewer than four times a year. (Exceptions to this norm may be in order for boards of nonprofit organizations that are multinational and have members living in widely separated parts of the world.)

Ironically, boards can also meet *too* frequently, thereby encouraging directors to act like managers or staff members, while simultaneously discouraging other potentially valuable candidates for board membership from serving at all. It is not always clear, however, what is cause and what is effect in such situations, since board members with intrusive instincts may press for more meetings, and for longer meetings. A colleague has observed that trustees with too much time to contribute can be just as problematic as trustees with too little time. She notes that trustees who themselves have much time available sometimes fail to understand the time pressures under which staff members work and cause staff time to be misallocated.

The theme of time is a recurrent one. A number of commentators have recommended that boards set aside enough time to allow directors to reflect on issues, to consider them once, and then to return to them. "Retreats" can offer useful opportunities for board members to get to know one another and to talk about longer term directions in a relaxed way. The amount of time that directors should be expected to contribute must be decided in conjunction with judgments about the ability of the board to recruit busy candidates, how board meetings are to be conducted, and what kinds of information are to be provided to board members.

Whatever time is available at board meetings must be used well. This requires careful preparation for meetings, with written materials mailed out well in advance. Directors should be informed of key topics on the agenda so that proper "mental preparation" can occur. While this admonition might seem unnecessary (and should be unnecessary), situations continue to arise in which directors are taken by surprise. Such oversights are hard to excuse if accidental, and more difficult yet to overlook if deliberate.

In planning meetings, careful attention to agendas and to board calendars can make a great difference. By paying attention to agendas, I mean more than just being sure that meetings are not consumed by routine reports, though that can be a problem in its own right. I endorse a suggestion by Taylor Reveley that board members themselves construct a different kind of "agenda": Individual directors would make lists of critical issues to confront in the course of a year; they could then consolidate those lists, reach agreement on central topics, and make plans to cover the topics in an orderly way.

The suggestion that board "calendars" be developed is analogous in many respects. One version of the idea—often associated with the Dayton-Hudson company, which produced a well-known board calendar in the form of a "wheel"—is that there be a planned sequence of topics covered during each year, with strategic planning followed by capital allocation, the development of long-range goals, performance appraisal, and manpower planning, leading back into another round of strategic planning.[13]

16 | Genuinely open discussion should be encouraged, regular use should be made of executive sessions, and there should be annual opportunities for directors to meet alone to review the performance of the CEO.

However skillfully materials are prepared and meetings planned, the consideration actually given to basic issues will depend on the character and quality of the ensuing discussion. This can be influenced significantly by attitudes and expectations. The CEO-chairman and other key directors can do a great deal to encourage open conversation, focused questions, and a willingness to try out ideas.

More boards seem to be making regular use of executive sessions, and this is a healthy development. Bruce Atwater,

CEO-chairman of General Mills and a leader within the business community in thinking about corporate governance, has emphasized this aspect of governance:

> Executive sessions are an essential complement to the presence of inside directors on the board [which he very much favors]. Boards ought to meet alone with the CEO and they ought to meet alone without the CEO. All of this is a package.

While everyone would hope for candor and uninhibited exchanges of ideas in settings in which the CEO and staff are present, the directors should have regular opportunities to meet alone. Executive sessions should be held as a matter of course, so that they do not seem strange or "special." The practice of asking "Has anyone got anything on his mind that we should discuss now" can encourage directors to be more open in expressing real concerns while simultaneously reducing the risk that they will simply brood over imagined problems.

In addition, the outside directors should meet periodically (at least once a year) to discuss candidly and in depth the stewardship of the CEO and any other relevant matters. The chairman of a committee on the board (or the chairman of the compensation committee) could take the lead in scheduling and chairing such meetings, so that they are seen as a regular part of corporate governance, not as occasions for awkwardness.

The Role of Independent Advisors

17 **The board should have ready access to advice from accountants, compensation consultants, lawyers, and investment bankers who are chosen by the outside directors, not by management.**

This goes without saying in the case of committees such as audit, which expect to meet regularly with external auditors who are responsible directly to the committee. Increasingly, compensation committees also expect to have direct access, at least periodically, to their own advisors, so that they can be confident they are receiving expert advice independent of that used to develop management's recommendations.

The intent of this norm goes beyond these conventional expectations. In complex situations, where much is at stake for all parties, standards of professionalism cannot be counted on to guarantee that experts hired by management will provide truly objective advice to boards that must evaluate proposals in which management may have a vested interest (and which the same advisors may have helped to formulate). In a world where litigation is so often a threat, boards are reluctant to go against the advice of a management-retained expert unless the board has advisors of its own who can counter the views expressed by others. Legal concerns of this kind, magnified by dire warnings provided by advisors retained by management, can be a major source of collective timidity. In critical situations (which presumably occur rarely), there is no substitute for having one's *own* advisors, who are there only to help the directors. I hasten to add that I am not suggesting lack of integrity among professional advisors (though that too can be a problem); rather, it is a matter of being sure that the key questions are being posed, and answered, from the board's own perspective.

This is another respect in which a separate chairman or the chairman of a committee on the board can be of great value. Without an established structure, it is difficult for outside directors to know how to go about retaining necessary advisors in special, highly charged, situations. Such needs are unlikely to be met promptly enough, if at all, by ad hoc procedures. While directors may hope they will never need to seek such special advice, it can be crucially important at moments of crisis. Most recently, questions have been raised about the advice available to the outside directors of Paramount when they were considering the competing bids offered by Viacom and QVC Network Inc. Some commentators have suggested that additional advisors, other than those selected by the CEO-chairman, should have been engaged.[14]

There are unusual situations in which nonprofit boards also need disinterested advice from experts, particularly if the organization is contemplating some radical change in its mission or structure and there is a risk of legal challenges. The case of Wilson College is again relevant. When the trustees attempted to close the college and redirect its assets to other purposes, alumnae and others objected strenuously, and a local court intervened to prevent the closing. Eventually, a consent decree was negotiated that called for the wholesale replacement of the board and a reconstitution of the college. Without judging the pros and cons of a complex situation, it seems likely that expert outside advice—especially legal advice—in the final stages of the process would have been helpful to the trustees.[15]

Management Succession

18 | **Every board should have in place some mechanism, formal or informal, for succession planning.**

This norm is satisfied routinely in almost all large, publicly-held companies. The usual practice is to use the compensation committee for this purpose, since there is a natural tie between reviewing the performance of the principal officers of a company and thinking about future roles for them. Also, it is customary, and desirable, for the compensation committee and the CEO to review succession plans and options with the full board.

The process of finding a new corporate CEO is only occasionally an easy one; in fact, it appears to be more difficult today than it used to be, perhaps because of increased specialization. As Richard Fisher, chairman of Morgan Stanley has observed, many capable people are "kept in small boxes" for a long time, and some of them are never given an opportunity to test themselves in large arenas until it is too late. This can be a problem even in well-run companies. One objective of an orderly succession planning process should be to minimize the risk that this will happen.

Nonprofits are much less likely to think systematically about succession planning. At one level, it is easy to understand why. These organizations tend to be less hierarchical and less likely to promote from within. While identifying and attracting outstanding leadership is just as important to nonprofits as to for-profit organizations, the next president or CEO of a nonprofit is quite likely to be recruited from outside the organization. For example, a study by the American Council on Education found that about one-third of newly elected college presidents were internal candidates, a fraction that remained amazingly constant when calculations were made for different types of institutions. According to a more recent ACE study, the overall percentage has now fallen to 28 percent.[16] When a search for a new CEO is undertaken by a nonprofit board, considerable time may be devoted to it; but discharging this responsibility is (everyone hopes) an episodic activity—in no way an ongoing function, as succession planning generally is within a corporation.

Nonetheless, it is my view that too often nonprofits, especially those founded or run for many years by charismatic leaders, devote little thought to the eventual need for a new president. When issues associated with succession are ignored until the search for a new leader must be launched, the search process itself may not go well. What often happens in the course of the search is that questions are unearthed that require answers prior to making a new appointment. The search may then be aborted or an outside advisor, such as a search firm, may be asked by the trustees to take on a consultative function that is not appropriate.

It would be better if, ahead of time, the boards of nonprofits thought through the institutional issues that precede the identification of a candidate. This process, which can be done quite informally, makes sense not because the new leader is likely to be found within the organization, but because a new leader can be recruited more easily if (in the words of one of my colleagues) "the institution is ready to be led." Nonprofit boards have a tendency to think that succession is more a personal issue than an institutional one: It is both.

19 | **While retiring CEOs should provide advice and counsel, responsibility for choosing a new CEO should rest squarely with the outside directors, not with the outgoing CEO.**

The arguments in favor of this proposition are much the same as the arguments for not retaining the former CEO on the board, especially the recurring need for a fresh examination of options and directions. Ironically, it may be easier, and more appropriate, for the retiring CEO to provide information and even strong advice concerning the selection of a successor if it is understood that the retiring executive is not going to continue on the board. Otherwise, board members may wonder about the extent to which self-interest is driving a CEO's recommendation concerning a successor. ("I know that 'Jones' will listen to me and see that my interests are protected.") The substantive case in favor of the candidate proposed by the retiring CEO is not helped when that question can arise.

A strong, independent role for the board in choosing a new CEO in no way relieves the previous CEO of the responsibility for nurturing a next generation of leadership within the organization. That obligation is present in any case. A CEO should always be concerned about succession and should work closely with the board in addressing that issue. The directors, in turn, should listen most carefully to the advice of the retiring CEO. It is hard for outside directors to have a nuanced sense of the qualities and capabilities of officers below the level of the CEO—who knows the strengths and weaknesses of those who worked directly for him better than anyone else. But it is entirely possible for the CEO to be helpful without presuming to have the last word. In my opinion, he should not. The new CEO should be chosen by the board—and should know from the start that that is where obligations reside and loyalties must be directed.

In the case of nonprofit organizations, it is usually taken for granted that the board will organize and conduct the search for a new leader. The nonhierarchial character of most nonprofits, their typically smaller size, the specialized skills represented by many of the leading staff members, and the lack of inside directors combine to mean that boards are unlikely to find a cadre of potential internal candidates competing for leadership. The retiring president may offer advice and meet with potential outside candidates, but it is almost always understood that the board, acting collectively, will make this important decision.

Why For-Profit Boards Are Organized Differently from Nonprofit Boards

Three of the central organizational norms that I have proposed reflect common practice among nonprofits, though not among for-profit corporations. Normally, in the nonprofit world: (1) an outside director, not the CEO, serves as chairman, (2) a new CEO is chosen by the board, not (de facto) by the retiring CEO, and (3) the retiring CEO leaves the board on retirement. In the corporate world, on the other hand, the opposite practices usually prevail.

Are there fundamental explanations for these sharp differences in the ways in which the two sectors structure relationships between the CEO and the board? What accounts, historically, for the presence of these very different traditions of governance? To focus on one specific question from the perspective of the nonprofit sector: Given the prevalence of the combined CEO-chairman model in the for-profit world, why do the CEOs of nonprofits so rarely chair their boards? This set of questions deserves more study than it has received. I have not done the research needed to provide anything like a full answer, but it may be helpful to speculate about some of the factors at work.

First, I suspect that practices in the nonprofit world owe a good deal to the long-recognized needs of these organizations for strong (and generous) external patrons. Managements of nonprofits simply could not survive on their own—as most managements of businesses could, and did, prior to the separation of ownership and management.[17] The existence of lay boards of trustees for colleges, museums, and hospitals has a venerable history tied to the American traditions of voluntarism and strong private-sector support of such activities. Unpaid volunteers often founded nonprofit entities, and it is hardly surprising that they have continued to play major roles in governance.

A second, related, hypothesis is that the public in general may have been—may be—more than mildly skeptical about the capacity of nonprofits to govern themselves (perhaps for good reasons). Many nonprofits reflect the interests of individuals who are idealistic, committed to a set of nonmonetary goals, and generally less experienced in some kinds of practical work than are those who live principally in the business world. These are stereotypes to be sure, and I have encountered both exceedingly practical (sometimes enragingly practical), business-minded people in nonprofit organizations and some truly otherworldly individuals working for large companies. Still, to the extent that the generalization holds, nonprofits need both the help and the stamp of approval that can be provided by the active presence on their boards of prominent business leaders, investors, lawyers, and statesman—with one such person usually serving as chairman. Potential donors may want assurances that boards are led by responsible, well-respected outsiders, who can be counted on to ensure that funds are invested wisely, that proper accounting practices are followed and, in general, that the enterprise is conducted in predictable, "certifiable" ways. (In Chapter 6, I raise questions concerning the degree to which these expectations are in fact satisfied by recruiting business executives to serve on nonprofit boards.)

Third, the distinctive missions of nonprofits have strong implications for organizational structure. In the case of colleges and universities, for example, the central importance of academic freedom and of academic judgments constrains the roles played by the president, other officers, and trustees. In such a setting, it is easy to see why a regularized, highly structured, hierarchial model of governance has little relevance.

More generally, the collegial structure of many classes of nonprofits, and the characteristics of their key staff members, imply the need for a strong external presence on boards. In most nonprofit organizations, it is assumed that many of the professionals on the staff (the faculty at a university, the curators at a museum, the doctors at a hospital) owe allegiance to their professions as well as to the particular institution for which they work.

Frederick Rudolph has described in detail the rise of "academic man" in the latter part of the 19th century, when faculty hierarchies and departments were established, publication was emphasized, learned journals and university presses were created, and sabbaticals for research became common. He writes:

> All this apparatus, all of these manifestations of organization, would be a tremendous boon to the academic itinerant, for whom a reputation in his profession was more important than any commitment to a particular institution. The tendencies of the new scholarship and of organization would make such a man loyal to professional

standards . . . but indifferent to the fate of the institution to which he might temporarily be attached. . . .

He goes on to suggest implications for governance:

> The professionalization of the professors had not brought them any new authority in college and university affairs; actually, it had only helped to widen the gap between them and the university board. . . . The structure of the colleges and universities in the end made room for an extremely professionalized faculty and for a governing board whose professional competence lay outside the main interest of the institution itself.[18]

These considerations help explain why the key actors in a nonprofit enterprise would be comfortable with a strong outside chairman, a dominant role for the board in choosing a new CEO, and reliance on the board itself and the institution overall, not on the outgoing CEO, to provide continuity. For-profit entities, in sharp contrast, often originated as creatures of either entrepreneurs or strong-willed managers and investors, and many evolved from family businesses. Internal directors were natural, since they were the ones who understood the business and had responsibility for running it. It was their money and their futures that were at stake. Thus, one can see why there would have been less of a sense of public accountability associated with business enterprises, and less reason to engage outsiders in overseeing their affairs.

Deeply rooted assumptions about how business leaders should comport themselves are also relevant. As one perceptive observer of corporations (William T. Allen, chancellor of the Delaware Court of Chancery) has put it:

> We tend to lionize the strong [business] leader, to associate efficiency with an organization animated by a decisive

person of action and vision, in whom ultimate power is entrusted. The military, more than the civilian government, seems to have been our model in practice.[19]

This is a real insight; it helps explain why there is such resistance to the idea of a separate chairman of the board within the business community. In nonprofits, there is a much stronger tradition of collegial decision making. Heads of nonprofits such as universities and hospitals are used to working with faculties and groups of doctors; they are more accustomed to sharing power and are less resistant to operating within complex decision-making structures.

We forget too easily that today's emphasis on the outside director is relatively new. It reflects major changes in patterns of ownership, and especially the rise of the large institutional shareholder. In addition, as one commentator stressed: "[It] is also part of today's pervasive distrust of the established order. . . . Now the public wants 'watchdogs' (or at least people with 'outside' perspectives and true independence) within the corporate sanctum."

My sense is that we are still trying to find the best ways to reflect legitimate shareholder interests in the oversight of large companies, and that experimentation will continue to be necessary. Some practices already common in the nonprofit world could prove useful to businesses as they seek to cope with this evolutionary process, and especially to find the right balance between the need for crisp decision making and the need for oversight. But I would not expect the precise organizational *forms* that have worked in the nonprofit sector to be carried over, without modification, to the corporate sector.

5

How Boards Are Informed

I didn't know enough, early enough." In talking with other directors about shortcomings, and in particular about our collective slowness in recognizing problems and dealing with them, this is the most common refrain. Examples are legendary. They extend from corporate cases to the widely discussed problems of the New-York Historical Society (see Appendix B). To be sure, directors of institutions in trouble will never feel that they were sufficiently well informed in advance of difficulties. It is so much easier to see what information should have been provided in retrospect than in prospect. Still, I would propose the following general norm, which is more injunction than anything else, as an essential prerequisite for productive discussions and informed decision making.

20 **Financial information and other measures of performance need to be presented clearly, consistently, and regularly, so that warning flags may be seen and serious problems anticipated.**

Timely access to the right information is an indispensable source of power in any institutional setting. Identifying the "right" information and finding the best formats in which to present it are large subjects all their own. They command the attention of more and more professionals (including political scientists, economists, psychologists, and other social scientists, as well as experts in business and in management information systems per se), and they deserve closer analysis than I can give them here.[1]

I will simply state two general propositions that frame my thinking:

1. Many nonprofits have great difficulty providing their board with adequate information; they have lessons to learn from the for-profit sector in this regard.

2. Granting the *relative* superiority of businesses in satisfying this norm, they too can do better in providing the most relevant data, which are by no means only financial.

Information for Corporate Boards

In general, corporate boards are considerably better informed than are nonprofit boards, particularly with regard to financial data and operating results. There are four primary reasons:

1. Corporations have more staff, time, and other resources available to summarize data and analyze trends.

2. The for-profit world has available to it numerous external "checks" that supply information to directors; in general, nonprofits have nothing comparable.

3. The usual monitoring and tracking exercises are better defined (easier) in the for-profit world: There are standard measures of performance (such as earnings per share, return on equity, and debt-capital ratios) that board members

understand and use regularly; in contrast, measuring "results" in the nonprofit sector can be an exceedingly difficult problem.

4. Accounting conventions used by for-profit entities are clearer and lead to more comprehensible financial statements than do the conventions used by nonprofit entities, especially those based on fund accounting.

The first point, concerning staff resources, requires no elaboration. Nor do I have anything of substance to add to what was said earlier (Chapter 1) concerning the greater availability of external checks in the for-profit sector. But I want to reiterate the importance to corporate directors of having access to information either required by regulators and rating agencies or generated by markets, securities analysts, and even reporters. While such information is never complete, and sometimes just wrong, it does raise valuable warning flags for corporate directors. In the main, nonprofit boards have no equivalent access to externally generated data. (Exceptions to this sweeping generalization include comparative data compiled by organizations such as the American Symphony Orchestra League and the American Association of Museums. Many other nonprofits have access to salary surveys and other "industry" data, which nonetheless fall far short of what is available routinely in most for-profit contexts.)

A key issue in the corporate arena is the extent to which the kinds of statistics regularly provided to directors adequately inform discussions and decision making. It is easy to become enamored of what appear to be precise measures of "performance" only to learn that the most important variables have been overlooked. Charles Exley has argued persuasively against exaggerating the value of the usual measures of performance unless they are accompanied by other information:

In managing a business, it has been my experience that one cannot depend on measures of performance alone in determining whether or not an individual should continue in his job. The reason . . . is that, surprisingly often, a manager getting good results is doing the wrong things and will ultimately fail as a consequence. It also happens, perhaps less frequently, that a manager producing poor results can be seen to be doing the right things so that he will ultimately succeed. This observation has led me to conclude that the board of a business needs to know enough about what the management is doing to be able to judge whether they are the right things or not. In the absence of this level of understanding, the board is not in a position to act until the results are very bad indeed—that is, until too late. . . . Monitoring results will never be sufficient as a means of evaluating the job being done by management.

Another keen student of business performance, Lewis Bernard, agrees with Exley. At a public meeting of the Competitiveness Council subcommittee on corporate governance, Bernard recalled that, in the 1930s, Moody's published a transportation manual containing reams of ratios against which railroads were to be judged. He then observed: "Almost every railroad met Moody's standards; virtually all, later, went bankrupt. Ratios cannot anticipate the future."

There is, without question, an emphasis in the business community today on supplementing the more narrowly based financial measures of performance with nonfinancial information, including qualitative indicators. Recognition of the limitations of purely financial measures is hardly new, but the idea seems to be enjoying a kind of renaissance.[2] Indicative is the attention given to this subject in the recent Report of the Subcouncil on Corporate Governance and Financial Markets to the Competitiveness Policy Council. This report notes that qualitative indicators of corporate performance such as quality of products, customer satisfaction, and employee training and morale are routinely discussed internally; it then calls for a "more systematic development of these measures" and identifies two projects of this kind now underway.[3]

Another generic problem exists in the corporate sector as well as among many nonprofits. The flow of information is limited by reticence on the part of some board members—by a reluctance or unwillingness to insist on having the data that are really needed. One commentator (Edgar Masinter of the law firm of Simpson Thacher & Bartlett) observed:

> I suggest that many boards may be less informed than they should be because of their unwillingness to press for information and in some cases because of the limited burdens that some directors are prepared to assume. Not all directors really work at the job. Also, "taking on faith," other business and personal relationships between directors and management, deference to status and the like can inhibit a dynamic exchange of information and views at the board level. Furthermore, management sometimes has a tendency to color information favorably or avoid reality. Boards can help rebalance these biases if they are willing to make the effort and be more inquisitive.

In the recent dispute at Paramount, comments by participants and observers alike suggest that the board was anything but aggressive in pressing for the information that it needed to assess both the appropriateness of various protections which it put in place and the value of the unwanted bid from QVC. For example, Judge Jacobs of the Delaware court said specifically: "The directors were not adequately informed as to whether the stock options would promote shareholders' interest in obtaining the best available transaction."[4]

It would be a mistake, then, to be overly enthusiastic about the accomplishments of corporate accountants and analysts in providing the most relevant data. Put more positively, we can applaud both self-recognition of shortcomings and efforts to do better within the corporate world. At the same time, the typical nonprofit organization faces analogous problems without having even rudimentary measures to use as a starting point for analysis.

Accounting Conventions in the Nonprofit Sector

Fund Accounting

Nonprofits suffer from an endemic disadvantage in seeking to assemble, understand, and communicate information about their financial health. They have to work within the framework of fund accounting. Anyone who has struggled with the mysteries arising from this arcane set of conventions will understand immediately what I mean. But I want to be fair in introducing the subject. It is important to understand, first, that fund accounting originated mainly out of a desire to assure donors and government agencies that their monies were being spent properly: in accord with the intent of the provider of the funds. It continues to serve this purpose.

It is equally important to recognize that many of the difficulties in understanding the finances of nonprofit entities stem from the inherent complexities growing out of the existence of restricted funds (typically gifts, grants, or endowments earmarked by donors for a specific purpose). This major complication cannot be laid at the door of fund accounting. In the case of a business, "revenue is revenue," and every dollar of revenue is available for the general purposes of the company. (The closest analogy to restricted funds is blocked currencies.) In general, there is no need to maintain innumerable special accounts or to worry that failure to achieve a precise coupling between a defined flow of restricted funds and a particular set of expenditures will cause serious problems, including legal ones. The need to keep track of "deferred revenue" adds additional layers of complexity for nonprofits.

The implications for presentation of comprehensible financial reports can be horrendous. To cite just one example, the audited financial statements for a recent year of a major nonprofit entity contained a "negative asset" of about $1.6 million under the "unrestricted current funds" column on a line called "Due (to) from other funds." When a colleague and I met with the president and chairman of the board, we asked them to explain this number, as well as some other puzzling transfers. They were as baffled as we were. Subsequently, the chief financial officer was able to explain the accounting conventions being employed. But surely there is something wrong when published, audited financial statements cannot be interpreted by key board members and officers other than the chief financial officer. More substantively, the serious budgetary problems of the organization in question were obscured during much of the 1980s by the treatment of realized gains on endowment, which were used to fund operating deficits.

These inherent attributes of nonprofits are by no means the only source of difficulty, however. The accounting profession cannot be said to have done all that it might have done to ease the most egregious problems. The two exposure drafts released in 1992 by the Financial Accounting Standards Board (FASB) and now adopted with minor modifications are helpful in some respects—for example by requiring the consolidation of certain accounts and the presentation of cash flows—but they are unhelpful in others, as we have tried to explain in detailed comments on them.[5] A central purpose of financial statements should be to facilitate understanding of the basic condition of the organization; it is not enough simply to satisfy technical reporting requirements and guard against fraud. In our view, progress to date in modifying accounting standards to meet this basic objective has been disappointing.

Two specific problems deserve emphasis. My colleagues and I believe, first, that there is no substitute for an operating statement. We regret that FASB has declined to require organizations to present such a statement. The reasons given center on inability to find a uniform way of presenting operating results. While this is no easy task, it is less important which specific conventions are adopted than that some set be chosen. In the absence of an operating statement, readers of financial reports will inevitably be driven to invent their own versions, and much confusion will result. It is all too easy to be misled, or to mislead.

A widely discussed series of newspaper articles in the *Philadelphia Inquirer* on the "wealth" of the nonprofit sector illustrates vividly what can happen in the absence of an operating statement. The articles apparently treat as "profit" the difference between the "Total Revenues" and "Total Expenses" lines on IRS 990 forms. This procedure leads to absurd results, such as the assertion that in 1991 the University of Pennsylvania "made $.11 in profit for each $1 it took in—$153 million profit on revenues of $1.3 billion." The authors seem to have failed to understand that the "Total Revenues" line on these forms often includes very large amounts of *noncurrent income,* which should be excluded from the usual measures of "profit." Examples would be a capital gift to build a new laboratory, a bequest to set up an endowed scholarship fund, or realized capital gains on permanently restricted endowments.[6]

A second problem has to do with returns on endowment. Policies adopted by governing boards regarding investments and spendable income generated by endowments need to be reflected in the basic financial statements of the organization. In this respect, the new FASB requirements are potentially very dangerous. All appreciation on invested funds must be reported as "unrestricted income for expenditure" unless the donor has imposed an explicit prohibition against the spending of appreciation (or the board of trustees interprets state law as imposing a similar restriction). The requirement that all other appreciation must be counted as unrestricted income applies even if an organization has adopted a spending rule that prudently limits, or "restricts," the drawdown on quasi-endowments.

This requirement can encourage imprudent spending by organizations (or, at the minimum, fail to discourage the practice). It can also mislead readers of financial statements concerning the long-term ability of the entity to sustain its current level of activities. Ironically, the problem is made even worse if an organization chooses to follow modern accounting trends and report its investments at market value. In that case, all *unrealized* appreciation (or depreciation) will also appear to increase or reduce the organization's "income," thereby generating substantial fluctuations from year to year solely as a consequence of market volatility.

Neglect of Capital Costs

The neglect of capital costs by many nonprofits raises other questions and creates a different set of confusions. Moreover, as Gordon Winston has pointed out repeatedly, financial reports are distorted because the *degree* of neglect of capital costs depends not just on how much capital an organization uses in its activities, but also on how it pays for whatever physical assets it has. As Winston shows, the cost of education at Williams College is grossly understated because the college owns its capital stock outright. "If Williams were to sell its campus to a private real estate entrepreneur and rent it back at a competitive rate, its apparent current costs per student would rise by almost 60 percent."[7]

In an earlier incarnation, it fell to me to renegotiate a contract between Princeton University and the U.S. Department of Energy (DOE) for the operation of the university's plasma physics laboratory. The DOE first refused to assign any value to the land used by the laboratory because the university owned it. The obvious solution appeared to be to sell the land and lease it back. A transaction of this kind would have satisfied the government's accountants, but it would also have been an absurd solution to a nonexistent problem. Sanity finally prevailed, and an agreement was reached that did not require this charade, though it was worded in such a confusing way that no trustee, reading the agreement, would ever have understood the basic economics of the arrangement.

In my view, Winston and others are entirely right in insisting that capital stocks be valued and that capital costs be recognized explicitly. This should be done whether an asset was acquired by purchase, received as a gift in kind, or leased. Otherwise, true costs are understated and potential trade-offs between different types of expenditures (current outlays versus investments in plant, for example) may be obscured.

The Need to Monitor Key Indicators

It is probably too much to hope, and unrealistic to expect, that accounting conventions can be modified sufficiently to address the needs of board members and others interested in understanding the finances of nonprofit organizations. A partial alternative is for organizations themselves, at the urging of their boards or at the initiative of their managements, to define and track "key indicators."

To illustrate, it would be useful for the board of almost any nonprofit organization to know the answers to the following questions:*

1. Is the institution in approximate financial equilibrium, from the standpoint of its operating statement?
2. Is the institution's capital base being eroded to pay operating expenses or to handle deferred maintenance? Is it growing fast enough to meet future needs?

---

*The indicators in this list are general ones, designed to apply to large numbers of nonprofit institutions. A list of this kind needs to be supplemented with other indicators that meet the specific needs of particular institutions.

3. What is the institution's fund-raising record, in regard to both current funds and capital gifts? How do its fund-raising results compare with those of similar organizations?

4. How vulnerable are the finances of the institution to changes in the circumstances or priorities of key donors? How diverse are the funders?

5. How does investment performance (in the case of institutions with significant endowments) compare with relevant benchmarks?

6. What de facto spending rate is being used, and is the reinvestment rate high enough to reflect institution-specific inflation factors?

7. Does the institution have sufficient liquidity and flexible funds to withstand temporary adversity? Does it maintain excessive cash balances?

8. How much debt is outstanding, and is it clear how the debt is to be serviced, if not retired?

Some of these indicators are easier to obtain than others. In the case of the return on endowments, Robert Kasdin, treasurer and chief investment officer at the Metropolitan Museum of Art, has observed:

> *Success is hard to attain but easy to evaluate.* At the end of each fiscal year the total return stares at the trustees and staff. Comparisons to other institutions with similar investment profiles are easy to conduct.

The investment function is perhaps unique in this regard among the activities customarily undertaken by nonprofits. (I am tempted to add that, within asset classes, failure is almost as hard to attain as success, given the "efficiency" of most financial markets—which is one reason more index funds are being used.)

Nonfinancial indicators are also very important, especially when they serve as indexes of that elusive concept, "output." For instance, a theater will want to monitor attendance, renewals of subscriptions, reviews of productions and other evidence of the quality of what it is producing, and perhaps also information concerning the composition of audiences and the educational consequences of its programmatic activities. Doctoral programs should monitor both the completion rates of graduate students and the time it takes those who earn degrees to complete their studies.*

The need for useful measures of outcomes is widespread, and the much publicized program for managing governmental services in Sunnyvale, California, is an example of what can be done by a public entity if there is the will to do it.[8] Apparently, the city has set performance standards of many kinds: Building permits are to be processed within 24 hours, graffiti must be removed from parks or public places with two days, 90 percent of emergency calls are to be answered by the police within five to six minutes, and so on. Bonuses are paid for achieving goals, and the process of monitoring progress in reaching them leads naturally to the analysis of the reasons for problems when, for example, police response time begins to decline.

---

*The lack of basic quantitative information, such as completion rates and time-to-degree, is extraordinary. While such data are hard to collect—much harder than might be imagined—more efforts along these lines must be made. Even more fundamental is information about the quality of the work that students complete and their subsequent career paths, though this is obviously more difficult to obtain.

John M. Harris, president and CEO of Rockefeller Financial Services, Inc., has provided a good example of the use that can be made of performance benchmarks in evaluating educational inputs: "When I was chairman of the Wharton Graduate Board, we established a set of benchmarks on incoming GMATs, grade point averages, student acceptances with joint admits to the Harvard Business School, and so on. These measures continue to be used today, almost 10 years later. This has really helped the School to focus on the issues of what kind of entering class they get. It also takes all the qualitative and defensive feelings of the staff out of the discussion."

Service-providing nonprofit organizations could benefit from studying this example from the governmental realm. Whatever the sector, there is much to be said for accepting the discipline of defining as many objectives as possible in clear-cut terms.

There remains the danger that those things which can be measured will be measured—and then given excess weight in assessing performance, as contrasted with less measurable factors, which may simply be ignored. In the case of colleges, too much attention can be paid to external awards won by faculty and too little attention given to the quality of teaching and the effectiveness of individual faculty members in supervising students. The Jones-Lindzey-Coggeshall analysis of the quality of graduate programs is a good example of a sophisticated effort to provide a series of "key indicators" intended to capture many different dimensions of graduate education and then to allow the user to decide which of some 15 different measures are most useful for the purpose at hand.[9]

There is no substitute for judgment in determining what constitutes a key indicator for a particular organization or a particular situation. This is far from an overwhelming disadvantage, however, since the very process of developing a list of indicators can be extremely productive. As Taylor Reveley has observed:

> Efforts to develop key indicators can be the occasion for a nonprofit board to think seriously (perhaps for the first time) about what really matters to the organization and about what it—the board—really needs to understand on a continuing basis in order to govern.

Ideally, the development of key indicators should be coordinated among similar entities so that data are collected in a way that permits appropriate comparisons to be made (as in the just-cited case of graduate programs). As noted earlier, the American Symphony Orchestra League has devoted a great deal of effort to compiling comparative data on many of the quantifiable aspects of orchestras of different sizes and types. Also, the American Association of Museums has taken an encouraging first step in this direction by publishing a report that includes organizational information such as dates of establishment, descriptions of program activities and admissions, and financial data such as sources of revenues. This report describes the findings of the first of what is planned to be a series of surveys undertaken because there simply was no national database for museums.[10]

In general, however, we have been disappointed to discover the large gaps in "industry" data that would benefit all the nonprofit organizations within a field. For example, it is difficult to obtain reliable time-series data on attendance within subsectors of the performing arts. Many individual organizations collect such data, but the service organizations do not appear to have found ways to assemble consistent data sets for their members over time. As a result, benchmarks are unavailable.

There is one serious attitudinal problem that should be acknowledged directly. My colleague, Rachel Bellow, warns:

> Some nonprofit arts organizations, particularly those that are "founder-driven," resist comparisons to "industry" standards even if such standards are applied in a nuanced, sensitive way. There is in these organizations a "cult of difference" that insists on the uniqueness of the enterprise, its *sui generis* mission, and that serves to flatter both the founding director and, by extension, the enlightened board of directors surrounding the director. It enforces a kind of "we/them" mentality between the organization and the field in such a way that when key indicators of failure surface, they are instead identified as failures of the "market" (which can at times mean the unenlightened funder, the red-meat-eating audience, the unimaginative consultant, and so forth). This perverse (and reminiscently adolescent) attitude—"I banish

you"—is particularly common among avant garde arts organizations.

It is fine for an organization to respect its heritage and to celebrate its special characteristics and distinctive contributions, but it will not do to refuse to place the organization in any broader context.

In talking with potential grantees in various fields, I have been struck often by the extent to which paid executives and board members have been surprised by great (and almost always unpleasant) "discoveries" about their organization and its prospects. I am absolutely persuaded that more determined efforts must be made to find simple, intelligible methods of tracking performance, watching closely for warning signals, and then utilizing the information needed to make tough decisions in a timely way. Otherwise, surprises will continue to plague these organizations, their directors, and all of us who depend on them and wish them well.

6

Business Leaders Serving on Nonprofit Boards

In this chapter I wish to consider a particularistic set of questions concerning the role of business executives serving on nonprofit boards. Is it true that well-regarded representatives of the business world are often surprisingly ineffective as members of nonprofit boards (somehow seeming to have checked their analytical apparatus and their "toughness" at the door)? If this is true in some significant number of cases, what is the explanation? And, what, if anything, can be done about it?

These questions are consequential precisely because it is so important that highly qualified individuals from "the world of affairs" serve effectively on nonprofit boards. They are needed for their knowledge, skills, and general competence. They are needed too for fund raising, for contacts more generally, and also for the sake of appearances. It is hard to identify a major nonprofit board that lacks business representation. I cannot think of any.*

Although it would be hard to devise a rigorous empirical test, I suspect that my initial, harsh-sounding proposition questioning the effectiveness of nonprofit board members from the business sector holds with surprising frequency. Having now checked this perception with a variety of individuals, I can report that it is widely shared. And, those endorsing this proposition include a number of members of nonprofit boards who are themselves from the business world. Commentator after commentator wrote alongside this section of the manuscript: "I agree," and then went on to cite examples (most of which are too personal to be given here).

There have also been a number of widely publicized cases. A story about the severe problems of Morris Brown College in Atlanta was titled "Financial Troubles at Small Black Colleges Raise Questions about the Role of Their Trustees in Overseeing Management."[1] The story quotes a new trustee as saying: "The board members did not do their jobs, period." It then goes on to point out: "The list of those that weren't doing the asking [of critical questions] includes some heavy hitters in Atlanta's business world. . . . In all, 15 of Morris Brown's 30 trustees were business professionals."

The business representatives on the United Way board certainly appear to have failed to do a proper job of overseeing the activities of that organization. Press accounts of the Empire Blue Cross debacle have referred regularly to the lack of proper oversight on the part of outside directors (who were a mix of health care professionals and individuals with business backgrounds), noting

---

*In my opinion, it is much more important that business executives serve on nonprofit boards than it is that individuals associated with nonprofit institutions serve on business boards. While we could also speculate on how effective academics and others from the nonprofit world are on corporate boards, that is a less important, and less interesting, question.

that board scrutiny did not adhere to the basic standards of the corporate world.

Needless to say, there are also a large number of instances in which my proposition about the performance of business executives on nonprofit boards does *not* hold. One commentator (Hanna Gray) observed that in her experience "[business] CEOs tend to be the *best* board members; they are more likely than others to understand how complex organizations function." I second this observation. At both Princeton University and the Mellon Foundation, trustees with extensive business experience have been highly effective. In short, the range of performance by business executives is very wide indeed, extending from "extremely disappointing" all the way up to "very best." Negative impressions are often so vivid, I suspect, precisely because they stand in such sharp contrast to counterexamples of truly outstanding performance.

Whatever the exact number of disappointing experiences, we have here a nontrivial phenomenon in search of an explanation.

Motives for Joining Nonprofit Boards

Motives for joining boards are certainly a relevant consideration. Without speculating on the varied reasons individuals join corporate boards (including, as one candid person put it, "lucrative rewards"), let me suggest that a number of individuals from the for-profit sector join nonprofit boards for reasons of status *and with the expectation* that they will be able to enjoy a kind of "vacation from the bottom line." Fortunately, many others (including some of the same people), join nonprofit boards because of deep personal commitments to their values and purposes.

Certain propositions follow if I am right in suggesting that at least part of the motivation for accepting membership on nonprofit boards is the enjoyment of membership in a new "club" (albeit one with potentially high dues when it comes time for trustees to make campaign contributions) that simultaneously provides a respite from morning-to-night struggles with earnings and balance sheets. Bitter struggle would mar the pleasure derived from such an association. It would also be marred by saying "no" to obviously meritorious requests for budgetary support—even when the condition of the financial statement, if it is understood, is problematic. I was told, for example, that the business members of the board of a private secondary school in severe financial difficulty nonetheless approved a request from a group of teachers for new equipment because "they just couldn't say 'no' to such dedicated teachers."

A related point is that some executives join nonprofit boards in part to shed the "barbarian" image that otherwise may afflict them—either in their own perceptions or in the perceptions of others. If the executive's objective is to soften that image, it will not do to play the part of the "bad cop" by insisting that the organization has to retrench, that it can't afford salary increases for abominably paid staff members, and so on. Listening to well-articulated statements of mission and providing vocal support even when that might seem imprudent can be a "nonbarbarian" way of behaving. This attitude, however, can militate against a board member's willingness to blow the proverbial whistle on extravagant, overly optimistic, even poorly conceived, proposals and financial plans.

The former director of a small arts organization has described another kind of situation in which differences in personal circumstances played a key role. She was earning a low salary as director of her organization, whereas her board members were, for the most part, wealthy individuals from the business world. Some board members plainly felt guilty about her low salary, and every summer they asked her why she didn't just "take the summer off." She would reply that there was work that simply had to be done and that if board members wanted to help, they could raise more money so that the organization could afford more support staff. Instead, board members attempted to assuage their sense of inequity by offering the hard-working, low-paid director certain privileges that were not healthy for the organization. Someone had to mind the store, as the trustees should have understood.

The consequences of too much "permissiveness" can be extremely serious, in part because other trustees may well defer to seasoned executives on the board when it comes to business matters. As one trustee from the academic world confessed: "I just assumed that if there were a serious financial problem, surely [Jones and Smith], with all of their corporate experience, would tell us." Unfortunately, "Jones and Smith" did not speak up, and the organization in question nearly failed—and may fail yet, since its fate is not settled. In retrospect, the board member from academia made a bad mistake in deferring to his business colleagues rather than trusting his own judgment about the seriousness of the financial problems confronting the institution.

Another motivation for joining nonprofit boards was cited by several commentators as a potential source of poor performance. As the head of one nonprofit organization explained, in reflecting on why people agreed to join boards such as his:

> Traditionally, the main motive was to perform a civic duty. . . . Now, there are "business interests" to be served. Some companies encourage (almost require) management members to serve on "x" outside boards, in part to develop business contacts.

A similar comment was made by Edgar Masinter:

> I have observed that many businessmen are on nonprofit boards because it is a way for their companies to encourage and indirectly be involved in public service. In other cases, the businessman board member helps with fund raising at the corporate level. United Way is probably a good example. I suspect that some United Way board members considered themselves as a financial proxy (i.e., corporate fund raiser) rather than a program and policy

participant and did not focus their primary attention on the overall role usually associated with board membership because that was not their commitment. It is clear that these same people would have been vastly more attentive to their overall role on a corporate board.

Other motives for joining boards represent a more general set of problems for certain classes of nonprofits. For example, the commendable desire of many graduates of colleges and universities to "give something back" can lead them to inject excessive doses of nostalgia into board deliberations. (People at Princeton used to call this the "furry Tiger" syndrome.)

Nonprofits of all kinds suffer from the presence of board members out to advance personal agendas. The former president of a foundation posed this question:

> What is it that tends to rush in to fill the vacuum left in nonprofits by the absence of a bottom line? My experience at [X] foundation left me jaundiced about this, for it seemed to me that human vanity and a desire to be kept excited about the wonders of the foundation were what rushed in. Too often, trustees wanted to be able to brag about what [X] is doing. . . .

While this can be a problem on corporate boards too, the need to focus on business outcomes is at least somewhat constraining.

Other Factors: Different Values, Fund Accounting, Distaste for Fund Raising, and the Nature of Key Issues

Many other factors affect how business leaders perform on nonprofit boards. Some may bring values to the board table that are simply inappropriate. One commentator cited a case in which a businessman on the board of a church kept pushing for "double-digit growth" no matter what the implications for the church's capacity to fulfill its real mission.

Another potential source of difficulty is that individuals familiar with corporate financial accounts may find it difficult to penetrate the intricacies of fund accounting. They are certainly far from alone in this respect. Yet, since they are presumed to be expert in such matters, they may be more embarrassed than most people to acknowledge that they don't quite understand the financial statements of the nonprofit entity.

I have also come to believe that reluctance to come to grips with financial difficulties can be due to a phenomenon noted in the earlier discussion of the reasons board members sometimes appear to lack courage. Concluding that an organization faces severe financial difficulties has consequences, often including the need to raise appreciably more money. If a board member does not want to participate actively in an aggressive fund-raising effort, the individual may be reticent to emphasize the danger signals revealed by the organization's financial statements. A linkage between failure to perceive signs of financial distress and lack of enthusiasm for new fund-raising tasks can be largely unconscious, but I suspect it is real, in at least some instances. It may just be more comfortable—easier—to draw down endowment, hope for a brighter day, and allow events to unfold. (Arjay Miller has suggested a golfing analogy: It is dangerous for a member of a golf club to complain about the greens, since he could then be made chairman of the greens committee.)

The Lack of Sanctions for Bad Judgment

On almost all nonprofit boards, if conditions become adverse, trustees can simply walk away. This may not be true if certain kinds of debt have been taken on and creditors are at the door, but even then assets are usually more than sufficient to discharge obligations. In addition, as was noted earlier, courts are reluctant to hold "volunteers" to a high standard of accountability.

The fact that individual trustees are rarely identified with troubled nonprofits, even in highly publicized situations, also makes it easier for them to disengage. Press accounts usually refer to boards as corporate bodies, sometimes naming the chairman but rarely any other members. Perhaps, as some have suggested, associating individual trustees more directly with the organizations that they serve would increase accountability; but I'm not sure how much difference it would really make. After all, a person's professional reputation as, for example, an investment banker, is not likely to be harmed by having served on the board of a struggling nonprofit entity, particularly if the trustee is perceived as having labored hard to save it. In contrast, prominent members of the board of a failed business undertaking can bear scars indefinitely. With less at stake, trustees of nonprofits may not look as closely at "the numbers," or pursue complex issues as doggedly, as they would have in a for-profit setting.

Unfamiliarity of Board Members with Critical Issues

A quite different kind of explanation for what may seem like either incompetence or indifference, when in fact neither is present, has to do with the missions served by many nonprofits. An unusually perceptive observer of the processes of decision making in nonprofits (Robert Kasdin, treasurer and chief investment officer at the Metropolitan Museum of Art) attributes many of the difficulties encountered by business trustees to their being asked to play roles that, in his words, "raise unfamiliar types of normative questions."

To illustrate, to what extent is a museum justified in exceeding an endowment spending limit in order to invest in a new conservation facility, library, or gallery? Informed decisions in such situations require a rather sophisticated understanding of the implications of *not* spending money, as well as of spending it, and a willingness to make hard intergenerational choices: What will be the long-term effects of either decision on the quality of the institution? On its value to scholars in the future? How does the trustee compare the benefits to be gained now (and into the future) through investments of this kind against the need to protect the core finances of the institution into the next generation by preserving the real value of the endowment?[2] Corporations also make present-versus-future choices all the time, but at least they have quantitative methodologies to guide them in framing the issues and projecting rates of return.

It is revealing to contrast the characteristics of another class of investment decisions made routinely by nonprofits: how to invest the institution's endowment. Portfolio decisions raise far fewer intractable issues and are much less controversial. Goals are easier to specify and the alternative means of pursuing them are better understood. It is hardly coincidental that board members who are professional investors or who otherwise have financial or business backgrounds usually function very well on the investment committees of nonprofits. The vocabulary is familiar, their skills are relevant, and there is little conflict over objectives.*

---

*This is hardly to say that no problems arise. This is an area in which conflicts of interest can be vexing and standards of propriety sometimes hard to enforce. As one observer put it: "Unfortunately, some trustees cannot consistently distinguish between their responsibilities as trustees and the temptation to invest the endowment as if it were their own. I also find an unattractive nepotism in which members of investment committees and investment managers reverse roles as they travel among institutions. The distance required for sound judgment disappears and the institutions are vulnerable to compromised performance." Some of these concerns are addressed by norms suggested in Chapters 3 and 4.

Staff Attitudes and Subtle Intimidation

If it is intrinsically difficult for any outsider to address normative questions that depend on a nuanced understanding of the mission of the institution and the choices before it, it is even harder to do so if the management and staff are unhelpful. And they can be unhelpful either inadvertently or willfully. A potential problem in some nonprofit organizations is that the professional staff may be so conscious of the unique qualities of their institution, and so sensitive to their own obligations to be the guardians of its uniqueness, that, perhaps unknowingly, they will patronize or even dismiss the "unwashed" executive. As one colleague (Jed Bergman) put it: "After all, this is *their* field; they are the ones who have studied the arts, or medicine, or science. And the more dire the circumstances, the more likely it is that members of the staff will feel a compulsion to 'save' the institution—even from the trustees."

The driving force is often not institutional loyalty alone. Many of the key employees of a nonprofit organization are professionals, who may well feel as much loyalty to their profession, and to the norms inculcated in them during their training, as they do to any particular employer. The consequence may be determination to hold a particular employer to what staff members regard as universal standards (regarding deaccessioning, for example, in the museum world), regardless of local conditions. Lay trustees, and especially those from the business world, may be considered, fairly or unfairly, insensitive if not ignorant in these respects.

A related attitudinal problem stems from the tendency for some individuals who have chosen to work in the nonprofit sector—at least in part because they respect its values—to harbor a thinly veiled hostility to the profit-making sector. Thus, if business leaders fear being perceived as ax-wielding barbarians, that fear may not be entirely unfounded. And such perceptions can lead staff members to phrase questions and to present information in such a way that there appears to be only one "right" answer.

Louis Gerstner, chairman and CEO of IBM and a member of various nonprofit boards, has observed another source of difficulty in obtaining information. He suggests that staff members in nonprofits are sometimes defensive and unresponsive because they are less used to constructive criticism than are staff members in corporations—which are more likely, he suggests, to have accepted a "culture of challenge."

A still more general problem can arise as a result of an odd kind of subtle (and at times not so subtle) intimidation that pushes in the opposite direction. High-achieving corporate representatives do not want to seem ill-informed, narrowly educated, or boorish by apparently failing to understand the reasons for an action that the nonprofit "pros" insist is essential. As a colleague who was a college president (Alice Emerson) recalled from her own experience: Some business executives on the board still thought of the faculty as "their teachers" and were most reluctant to argue with them.

Needless to say, by no means all board members, whatever their backgrounds, are so reverent! In fact (and this is the other side of the attitudinal coin), some have been known to display more than a little contempt for "impractical intellectuals." The healthiest relationships, at least in my experience, exist between board members and staff members who genuinely respect each other. This is obviously easier if the board member from the business world has some real understanding of the fields served by the nonprofit organization.

A commentator who has served on, and worked with, the boards of a number of community service organizations (Frederick Borsch, Episcopal bishop of Los Angeles) has emphasized the need for trustees to understand the laborious, time-consuming ways of making decisions that often characterize these nonprofit organizations. In Bishop Borsch's words: "Some businesspeople are poor board members of nonprofits because they can't stand the slower, more collegial, pace of decision making. They want everything settled *now.*"

The point of these comments is most certainly not to criticize members of nonprofit boards who come to their posts from successful careers in business: They are badly needed. Rather, the intention is to warn unsuspecting leaders of nonprofit organizations, other board members, and staff members not to assume that those directors with business qualifications will necessarily contribute the same kind of hard-nosed approach in this setting that they are known to exhibit regularly in their professional lives.

There is much that the management and staff of nonprofit organizations can do to facilitate more effective participation by business executives in discussions of priorities, resource allocation, and financial planning. There should be a conscious effort to make board reviews and board deliberations as "trustee-friendly" as possible. This involves making a genuine attempt to demystify the central issues and to talk candidly about trade-offs. Also, ways need to be found to encourage board members with business experience to be just as disciplined, perhaps even more disciplined, in assessing the condition of a nonprofit organization as they would be in a profit-making setting. "Tough love" is necessary here every bit as much as it is needed in other contexts in which "good intentions randomize behavior."[3]

This injunction, however pertinent, is often ignored in nonprofit contexts for a reason stated by Frederick J. Kelly, former dean of the School of Business at Seton Hall University:

In working with a lot of agencies that "do good," I find a feeling from the employees on up through the board that because we are "doing good" some *deus ex machina* will always save us from having to make the hard decisions. Obviously this is not true. However, until the problem becomes clearly recognized, usually in a true crisis, people merrily wait for "God to provide."

I can certainly relate to this observation, having once been charged with examining the finances of Shelton College in Cape May, New Jersey, an institution led by the Reverend Carl McIntyre. When I pointed out to Reverend McIntyre that expected expenses seemed to be much higher than expected income, he replied, in effect: "Yes, I can understand how you would think that. However, the Lord will provide." The only response I could manage was: "That may well be true, but it would be nice to have some sense of the mechanism."

Mechanisms matter, and experienced business executives have much to contribute by insisting that fine motives and high hopes are not enough. It is necessary to have at least some sense of what is in fact likely to happen—and then to make the difficult decisions accordingly. Good intentions do randomize behavior.

Conclusion

I have written this small book in part because of a desire to emphasize what a challenge it is to be a good director of *any* enterprise, in the for-profit or nonprofit sector. Needed are not only competence and dedication, but also courage and empathy, open-mindedness, and a capacity to work in organizational settings in which the distribution of authority is ambiguous and personal relationships are complex. Managing an organization is generally much easier.

In the for-profit world, the overarching issue facing boards is how to achieve a sensible balance between mechanisms that encourage crisp executive decision making and mechanisms that encourage the right kinds of oversight by governing boards. Many of the norms I have proposed are intended to improve this balance. In my view, it is often tilted too much in the direction of the CEO.

I do not believe, however, that the right way to redress the balance is by setting out to "defang" the chief executive. CEOs need to be strong leaders. They should be expected to come to clear conclusions, to advocate decisive steps, and to act. It would be counterproductive to encourage CEOs to be less aggressive, to hang back, to be more passive. It is the other side of the equation that requires attention if a better balance in the distribution of responsibility is to be achieved: *The real need is for boards to be less supine.* Boards should be reliable sources of constructive skepticism, and board members should be good critics as well as compatriots. Strong CEOs and strong boards can complement each other in any number of ways, and both are necessary for an enterprise to function at its best. A healthy, friendly, tension is appropriate.

Experiences in the nonprofit sector convince me that more of a partnership approach would benefit companies and their CEOs. And I also believe that directors of for-profit enterprises could be more effective participants in corporate governance—better partners—if more appropriate organizational structures and expectations were in place. In designing mechanisms, and in reformulating unspoken norms, there is much room for creativity. What works well in one situation may work imperfectly, if at all, in another that looks the same but is in reality quite different. For this reason, I have stated my norms in rather general terms and have emphasized that they are presumptive only.

Whatever the structure, there is an overriding need for directors to possess "the will to act." In the absence of directors with courage, no hard decisions will be made. This is the thesis articulated repeatedly by Bruce Atwater, among others, and he is right to give it such emphasis. But it would be a mistake to stop with this proposition.

The key point, from my perspective, is that *governing arrangements make it either easier or harder to exercise courage:* Organizational forms, established processes, and informal conventions all make an enormous difference in this regard. Well-conceived mechanisms give outside directors the opportunity to nominate (and replace) their colleagues, influence the construction of board agendas, participate actively in setting strategic directions, monitor the performance of management, ensure the absence of conflicts in the conduct of the business, and discuss candidly the leadership provided by the CEO. Providing such opportunities makes it much easier for directors to be effective.

I am also convinced that "up-front" investments of the time and energy needed to put good mechanisms in place can pay large dividends. Once sound structures have been adopted, and once directors (and management) become accustomed to using them, concern about governance can recede into the background, as it should. The whole point, after all, is to create machinery that allows directors to focus on *substance* and not to be preoccupied with process. Governance is a means to an end, not a thing to be admired in and of itself. Ironically, it is the lack of attention to governance that is most likely to create situations in which debates about decision-making processes are time consuming, intense, and distracting. The objective, then, should be to have in place a system of governance that satisfies reasonable norms and that operates routinely and (in appearance at least) more or less effortlessly.

The guiding principles and practices must be more than implicit, however. It should be made hard for directors to forget to do the right thing. To illustrate what I mean, I have been in meetings of nominating committees in which the CEO remained throughout the deliberations because no one (including the CEO) "remembered" that the outside directors were supposed to have an opportunity to talk alone about potential nominees. Being explicit about such important conventions reduces awkwardness and increases the odds that responsibilities will be discharged appropriately. As a physicist-friend (Aaron Lemonick) used to say in another context: "If it goes without saying, it should definitely be said." Or, alternatively: "If you think everyone already knows it, be sure to write it on the blackboard." That is wise counsel.

A theme of this book is that nonprofit boards and for-profit boards have much to learn from each other. I am also persuaded, however, that fundamental differences between the two sectors are so profound, and so connected to distinctive missions, that no simple transplants of "best practices" are likely to work well. While there are unifying principles of governance—common norms—applications need to be tailored to the circumstances of the two sectors, and, for that matter, to the still more particularistic needs of numerous subcategories of institutions within each sector.

It seems to me especially hard to be an effective director of a nonprofit organization. The very mission of the enterprise can be difficult to define with precision and subject to intense debate. It is often seen differently by various influential participants and supporters. Relevant data and analyses are frequently either unavailable or, if available, slippery to the interpreter's touch. Resources are almost always scarce, and substantive problems can be both daunting and apparently intractable. Creative solutions are often elusive and, if identified, hard to put into effect—in part because of the lack of ready access to the kinds of "buy-sell" mechanisms provided by markets. These conditions often result in assigning too high a value to historical continuity and institutional survival per se.

Performance often defies easy assessment, and lackluster leadership can go unnoticed for considerable periods of time. As in the corporate world, CEOs can be given both too much leeway to make serious errors and too much opportunity to rest on their laurels. At the other extreme, nonprofit boards are more likely than corporate boards to be tempted to do the CEO's job for him (sometimes because of excess diffidence on the part of the CEO). In this sector, finding the appropriate balance between executive authority and board oversight is more likely to require strengthening the hand of the CEO than building up the powers of the board. CEOs in the nonprofit sector are sometimes too reluctant to lead and, if need be, to take on their boards. Perceptive board members may themselves recognize a situation of this kind but not find it easy to correct.

The obverse side of these sober-sounding observations is that nonprofit boards are tremendously important. They can have more impact on the success or failure of an organization than can most for-profit boards. There is more "room" for judgments to be made, good and bad. In the nonprofit world, there are multiple objectives for boards to weigh, each involving options having to do with purposes and priorities as well as the means to be followed in achieving defined ends. External signals are less numerous and less distinct. Outcomes are often indeterminate.

This is certainly not meant to be anything like a message of despair. One of the hallmarks of our society is the number and vitality of nonprofit entities. In their own ways, they have much to teach their profit-making relatives about the marshaling of resources, how to do much with little, and the advantages of forms of collegial decision making. Their continuing success depends in no small measure on the willingness of talented people to work diligently on their behalf as directors or trustees. Since monetary rewards are modest at best, and usually nonexistent, we can be grateful that so many people seem genuinely to believe that working hard for a good cause is its own highest reward—and a privilege. That is, let me say emphatically, my own view.

Appendix A

Presumptive Norms

1. The size of for-profit boards should normally fall within a range of, say, 10 to 15 members; many nonprofit boards should be larger—in the range of, say, 12 to 30, with even larger sizes justified in some circumstances.

2. Inside directors can be highly valuable members of boards, and the CEO should not be the only insider; but the number of insiders should be strictly limited—outside directors should predominate.

3. Selection of exceptional individuals to serve as outside directors is of paramount importance, and courage and empathy are key qualities that should be emphasized.

4. The board of every organization should contain several outside directors with particular knowledge of its genre.

5. Diversity of both backgrounds and perspectives is important in composing a board, but it needs to be achieved without sacrificing agreement on a common set of assumptions about the institution and its mission.

6. In selecting board members, care should be taken to avoid "incestuous" relationships and to preserve a certain amount of distance between board members and the CEO.

7. A former CEO should not continue to serve on the board, except in rare cases and (at most) for a short time.

8. Board members should serve defined terms, with upper limits on consecutive years of service; mechanisms should exist for monitoring the performance of board members and assuring turnover.

9. Compensation of directors of for-profit corporations should be reasonable, and board members should receive no additional compensation beyond that provided for service on the board itself: There should be no additional consulting fees or other special benefits.

10. Directors of certain classes of nonprofits (those that provide services but do not seek contributions) should also be compensated; but directors of "charitable" nonprofits, which seek contributions from others, should contribute their own services.

11. The board should have either a nonexecutive chairman or an alternative structure (such as a strong committee on the board led by an outside director) that will allow the board to discharge its obligations without usurping managerial functions.

12. Committees should not make major policy decisions for the board as a whole.

13. Committee structures should reflect the needs of each organization and should facilitate the exercise of independent judgment by outside directors, including the nomination of new directors.

14. The chairman of the compensation committee should be a resolutely independent soul, and no one director should occupy that position for very long.

15. Boards should meet with reasonable frequency, and board agendas and board calendars should assure time for discussion of the most important topics.

16. Genuinely open discussion should be encouraged, regular use should be made of executive sessions, and there should be annual opportunities for directors to meet alone to review the performance of the CEO.

17. The board should have ready access to advice from accountants, compensation consultants, lawyers, and investment bankers who are chosen by the outside directors, not by management.

18. Every board should have in place some mechanism, formal or informal, for succession planning.

19. While retiring CEOs should provide advice and counsel, responsibility for choosing a new CEO should rest squarely with the outside directors, not with the outgoing CEO.

20. Financial information and other measures of performance need to be presented clearly, consistently, and regularly, so that warning flags may be seen and serious problems anticipated.

Appendix B

Capsule Profiles of Selected Organizations*

This appendix provides readers with basic background information on four for-profit and five nonprofit organizations cited in the text to illustrate general points. Each summary includes features of the recent histories of the organizations. We do not purport, however, to assess the events in question, and this brief commentary is not meant to be judgmental. Citations are provided to the reports in the press that have been the main sources for these profiles.

For-Profit Companies

American Express

On January 29, 1993, James D. Robinson III announced his resignation as CEO and chairman of American Express. His

---

*This appendix was prepared by Joan Gilbert.

resignation followed a series of contentious board meetings and resulted in part from pressures exerted by institutional shareholders as well as some employees and outside directors. Prior to Robinson's resignation, three directors resigned in the aftermath of the meeting of the board held on January 25, when it appeared that Robinson would continue to serve as chairman, though not as CEO. All these events were widely reported in the press.

In recent years, American Express experienced a number of setbacks, including losses in its Optima division, pressures on margins and market share in its core credit-card business (resulting in part from increased competition from other cards), and problems stemming from what was regarded as the ill-fated acquisitions of Shearson-Lehman and Hutton. In addition, there was an unsuccessful attempt to orchestrate a leveraged buyout of RJR Nabisco.

At the January board meeting, Harvey Golub, who had been president, was elected CEO to succeed Robinson. Then, following Robinson's subsequent resignation as chairman, an outside director, Richard Furlaud, was elected to that post. Under Golub's leadership, the retail part of Shearson was sold to Primerica in July 1993. Other measures were taken to restore stability, improve earnings, and cause analysts to look more favorably on the company; the share price rose appreciably. At the board meeting in July 1993, a new president was elected and Golub was given the additional title of chairman, replacing Furlaud in that role; Furlaud was named chairman of the executive committee.

Sources: Jay Mathews, "American Express's Chief to Step Down; Coup Report Denied," *Washington Post,* December 6, 1992, A31; Kathleen Day and Brett D. Fromson, "Meeting May Have Sealed CEO's Fate; At American Express, A Closed-Door Session," *Washington Post,* December 7, 1992, A20; Jolie Solomon et al., "Jimmy Leaves Home," *Newsweek,* December 21, 1992, 50; Allen R. Myerson, "American Express Chairman Quits after Days of Corporate Turmoil," *New York Times,* January 31, 1993, Section 1, 32.

Eastman Kodak

Kodak is another old, highly regarded company that found itself in serious difficulty in the early 1990s. A principal issue was the adequacy of the cost-cutting measures that the company was making to improve its market share and increase its profitability. The Fuji Photo Film Company and private-label producers had cut into one of Kodak's main sources of income, and its copier business had also lagged behind that of some of its competitors. In recent years, profits failed to rise above the 1988 peak of $1.4 billion.

Pressures for changes in management were intensified when Christopher J. Steffen, who had been appointed chief financial officer in February 1993 to lead cost-cutting efforts, resigned abruptly amid reports he had clashed with the chairman and CEO, Kay R. Whitmore, a Kodak veteran and supporter of consensus management. Within three months, Whitmore was dismissed by the board and a search was launched for a new CEO who, it was announced publicly, would come from outside the company. Outside directors described as pressing for new leadership included Coca-Cola chairman and CEO Roberto C. Goizueta and former New York Stock Exchange chairman John J. Phelan, Jr.

Sources: Jay Mathews, "Kodak Ousts Chairman, A Company Veteran; Directors Say They Want Faster Cost Cutting," *Washington Post,* August 7, 1993, B1; Richard Cohen, "Lives—Not Profits," *Washington Post,* August 24, 1993, A17; Annetta Miller et al., "Picture This Executive Battle," *Newsweek,* May 10, 1993, 54.

General Motors

General Motors was one of the first major companies to revamp its board structure and to elect new leadership in 1992. It has been widely cited as an exemplar of "Rebellion in the Boardroom" (*Newsweek,* April 20, 1992, 58). The GM board was led by outside director John Smale, retired chairman and CEO of Procter & Gamble, who first replaced Robert Stempel as chairman of the executive committee in April 1992 and then was elected chairman of the board in November 1992. Stempel had replaced Roger Smith as CEO just two years earlier; Smith remained on the board at that time but subsequently also resigned as a director—under pressure from some outside directors and large institutional shareholders, according to press reports. Stempel was replaced as CEO by John F. Smith, Jr., on November 2, 1992.

These changes came following a prolonged period of difficulties for GM, as it tried to find a strategy that would regain its leadership role in the automotive industry. The company registered a $4.5 billion loss in 1991 and an operating loss of $2.7 billion in 1992. Benefiting from improved efficiency in auto making and a strong performance from its nonautomotive subsidiaries, GM posted an $889 million profit in the second quarter of 1993, compared with a loss of $703 million in the corresponding period a year earlier.

Throughout this process, the board of GM has been advised by Ira M. Millstein, a prominent attorney at Weil, Gottschal and Manges who is well known for his advocacy of the separate chairman model. At this writing (December 1993), GM, unlike American Express, continues to have a chairman separate from its CEO.

Sources: John Schwartz et al., "GM's Shake-up Shows the New Muscle of Directors," *Newsweek*, April 20, 1992, 58; Jolie Solomon et al., "One More Pink Slip," *Newsweek*, November 2, 1992, 70; Doron P. Levin, "Fast Action Called Key for G.M. Board Meets Today to Name New Chief," *New York Times*, November 2, 1992, D1; Jeanne B. Pinder, "G.M.'s White Collar Staff Is Offered a Novel Buyout," *New York Times*, February 20, 1993, 33.

IBM

One of the most highly respected corporations in the world, IBM was hurt badly by rapid changes in technology—specifically by the rapid development of distributed processing and the growing interest in "open systems." It was not easy for IBM to move away from its dependence on mainframes, which had been the primary source of its dominant position in the industry.

The company was under great pressure from institutional investors and from the business press to make changes in both its business and its leadership, and in January 1993, John F. Akers resigned as chairman and CEO. The board was led by an outside director, James E. Burke, retired chairman and CEO of Johnson & Johnson, as it searched vigorously and publicly for a new CEO. The search, which was marked by the joint participation of two leading executive search firms, Heidrick & Struggles and Spencer Stuart, culminated in the election of Louis V. Gerstner as chairman and CEO. Gerstner had been chairman and CEO of RJR Nabisco and, before that, president of American Express.

Since his election, Gerstner has sought to restructure the company, though without breaking it up, as some had predicted he would do. Also, there have been a number of management changes as well as changes in board membership and structure. In 1993, the company established a board committee composed entirely of outside directors to focus on corporate governance (Chapter 4).

Sources: John Schwartz et al., "Available: One Impossible Job," *Newsweek,* February 8, 1993, 44; Judith H. Dobrzybski, "IBM's Board Should Clean Out the Corner Office," *Business Week,* February 1, 1993, 27; Michael W. Miller, "IBM Overhauling Its Board, Will Create Governance Panel of Outside Directors," *The Wall Street Journal,* July 30, 1993, A1.

Nonprofits

Empire Blue Cross and Blue Shield

For most of its 60-year history, the network of national nonprofit companies known as Blue Cross has maintained a reputation of putting service before profit and offering health insurance to anyone who wanted it, at the lowest possible cost. In the 1990s, however, there have been mounting indications of difficulty, as large losses have been reported and premiums have risen rapidly. Requests for large rate increases stimulated questions about the quality of management, and there was increasing skepticism about claims by Blue Cross that its problems were due primarily to competitors skimming off the most lucrative business and leaving Blue Cross with those whom no one else would insure.

A Senate Committee began investigating the network, and Empire, the largest of the plans, came under special scrutiny. In June 1993, U.S. Senate investigators delivered a severe indictment of many aspects of the operation of Empire, asserting: "Gross mismanagement, wasteful expenditures, fraud, and a history of inattentiveness and nonaction by its board of directors and the State Insurance Department have made it critically ill" (Dean Baquet, "U.S. Finds Cheerleading in Monitoring of Empire," *New York Times,* June 26, 1993, 24).

Earlier, the press in New York had been making similar comments, noting apparent instances of conflicts of interest, including the awarding of computer business to a board member. The chairman and CEO, Albert A. Cardone, then resigned under fire. An interim chairman, Harold Vogt, was elected in May 1993, and Vogt was in turn replaced by Philip Briggs in July 1993. A new CEO, G. Robert O'Brien, was subsequently recruited from outside the company. Even more recently, an internal investigation has confirmed that the company kept two sets of books, one intended to make the case for large rate increases.

There has been much discussion of inattentiveness of board members (including a lead editorial in the *New York Times* titled "The Sound of Snoring at Empire," August 21, 1993, Section 1, 18), and one of the issues raised by this case is whether directors of service-providing nonprofits of this kind should be "volunteers" (Chapter 3).

Sources: Dena Bunis, "Empire Finance Officer Faces the Ax; Board Meets on His Fate Today," *Newsday*, July 15, 1993, 43; [Editorial] "The Failure to Police Empire," *New York Times*, July 2, 1993, A14; Jane Fritsch, "At Empire, the Glow of Greed," *New York Times*, Section 4, 20, July 11, 1993; Martin Gottlieb, "For Nation's Blue Cross Plans, Echoes of the Troubles at Empire," *New York Times*, August 2, 1993, A1.

Heye Foundation (Museum of the American Indian)

In the early 1900s, New York-born George Gustav Heye established a museum for arts and artifacts of the American Indian; the Heye collection is recognized today as the greatest one of its kind. Unfortunately, after its founding in 1916, the museum languished for decades. The Heye Foundation was unable to care for it properly: The collection was poorly maintained in a space that was inadequate to the size and quality of the collection, and the location discouraged some potential visitors from coming to see it.

Following a long period of neglect, the situation came to a head in the mid-1970s. In 1974, a museum trustee, Dr. Edmund Carpenter, charged the director, Dr. Frederick J. Dockstader, with mismanagement and selling off items from the collection. The attorney general of New York ordered an inventory of the museum collection as part of a general overhaul of its administration. Dockstader and all trustees except Carpenter resigned. With the museum now in the public eye, strenuous efforts were made to save it, and to keep it in New York, in accordance with the deed of gift. Options included maintaining the collection at its location on Audubon Terrace, moving it to the Custom House (a federal building in lower Manhattan), or merging it with the American Museum of Natural History. At one point, Ross Perot offered to build a $70 million museum for the collection near Dallas, Texas.

Eventually a decision was made to entrust the entire collection to the Smithsonian Institution, with the understanding that a new National Museum of the American Indian would be built on the Mall in Washington, D.C., and that a satellite museum would be established at the old U.S. Customs House in lower Manhattan so that the collection would still have a presence in New York. Congress passed the necessary legislation in November 1989, and efforts are now being made to raise the funds needed to build the new museum on the Mall.

Sources: Amei Wallach, "Pathways to Indian Insight: A Native American Exhibit Answers the Columbus Hype with a 'We Have Always Been Here' Point of View," *Newsday,* November 13, 1992; Heidi L. Berry, "In Pursuit of Native American Art: As Aesthetic Appreciation Increases, So Does the Value of Indian Artifacts," *Washington Post,* November 23, 1989, T9; Kara Swisher, "Indian Museum Board Picked," *Washington Post,* January 27, 1990, C9; Elizabeth Kastor, "Smithsonian Accepts Indian Museum Plan; Regents Vote 'in Principle' for Mall, Manhattan Sites," *Washington Post,* January 31, 1989, D3.

New-York Historical Society

Established in 1804, the New-York Historical Society has vast holdings of art, artifacts, books, manuscripts, and other documents about life in colonial America, and in New York in particular. While the Society's holdings are valued in the billions of dollars, it has been unable to balance its operating budget for a number of years and ran so short of cash that it had to close its doors in February 1993.

In fact, the finances of the Society have deteriorated over decades, with the endowment depleted to cover recurring deficits. In June 1988, the trustees closed two floors of galleries and dismissed almost a quarter of the staff. After news of the deterioration of parts of the collection became public, the director resigned. In several instances, holdings were sold on the private market to raise money for operations. In July 1988, after reports in the *New York Times* that hundreds of paintings owned by the Society had suffered severe deterioration in a warehouse in New Jersey, the New York State attorney general began an investigation of the society's stewardship of its collection, as well as its financial management.

With a largely new board and a new president, Barbara Debs (who had been a board member), the Society undertook a systematic inventory of its collections and raised more than $22 million during the next few years. Nonetheless, severe financial problems persisted, as it proved difficult to raise funds for general operating support. Repeated efforts to obtain aid from the city and state were unsuccessful.

Barbara Debs resigned as CEO in October 1, 1992, having served longer than she had originally intended; at this writing the Society is led by two board members (both investment bankers), Wilbur L. Ross and Herbert S. Winokur, who are serving as co-CEOs. The Society obtained a loan from Sotheby's to be used as bridge financing (with objects from the collection put up as collateral), and commitments were obtained from the city and state to help meet both capital needs and operating costs.

Over the past half dozen years, a number of discussions about merging parts of the Society with other city institutions failed to come to fruition. Most recently, however, New York University has agreed to manage the library on at least an interim basis, and the collections are now open again to scholars and other visitors. It is too early to know if the new plan will succeed; the future of the collections must still be regarded as unclear.

Sources: Michael Kimmelman, "Is This the End for New York's Attic?" *New York Times,* February 21, 1993, Section 2, 1; William Grimes, "Historical Society Gets N.Y.U.'s Help," *New York Times,* August 12, 1993, C13; [Editorial] "Now Fix It Up," *Newsday,* April 5, 1993, 34; William H. Honan, "Historical Society Tries to Live by Subtraction," *New York Times,* March 12, 1993, C3; Douglas C. McGill, "Panel Will Seek Rescue for Historical Society," *New York Times,* August 14, 1988, 36.

United Way

In February 1992, after the *Washington Post* had questioned the management practices and personal spending of William Aramony, the president of United Way of America, the board accepted his resignation. Initially, Aramony's problems were characterized as "sloppy record keeping." The board sponsored an investigation and several months later released a report by an external group alleging a pattern of financial misconduct over several years including the diversion of money to questionable spinoff organizations run by longtime aides of the president. Other disclosures revealed undocumented travel costs incurred by the president of over $100,000 between 1988 and 1991.

The widely reported abuses in the United Way case were particularly surprising to many people because the board was composed of a number of highly regarded executives, including John Akers of IBM, who was its chairman. In the wake of the disclosures, changes have been made in both the management and the board. A new CEO, Elaine Chao, was appointed. She has an MBA from Harvard, ran the Peace Corps, and was a deputy secretary in the Department of Transportation. As part of the effort to provide greater oversight, the board of governors has been expanded from 37 to 45 members and its membership now includes, for the first time, local United Way leaders. Six new board-level committees have been added, including ethics, finance, and budget. These committees are also made up of new members. All told, of the 103 people on the board and on board-level committees, 75 percent are now from local United Ways.

Still, United Way has been struggling to regain respect and support. For the first time since World War II, the organization reported a 4.1 percent drop in contributions to its 1992–1993 fund-raising campaign.

Sources: Nanette Byrnes, "The Nonprofit Business," *Financial World,* August 3, 1993; Felicity Barringer, "United Way Says Slump and Scandal Are Bringing Sharp Dip in Donations," *New York Times,* November 20, 1992, A14.

University of Bridgeport

The University of Bridgeport evolved from the Junior College of Connecticut and was chartered as a four-year institution in 1947, when it assumed its present name. After rapid expansion in the 1960s, enrollment hit a high of over 9,000 in 1969. During the 1970s, the administration and faculty sought to expand the graduate program, but for a long time did not realize that it took four to five part-time graduate students to pay tuition equal to what one full-time undergraduate paid. Many of the graduate students were foreign, with an especially large number of Iranian students, which made enrollment vulnerable to political changes worldwide. The city of Bridgeport itself (like many similar cities) was deteriorating, and the perception of crime discouraged students, especially women, from enrolling. By 1986, the number of new full-time undergraduate students had dropped to 658, down from 1,024 in 1984. Sizable deficits were run and substantial debt was incurred. The university attempted to resolve financial strains through faculty layoffs, but triggered a strike instead.

Several colleges and universities in Connecticut were approached to merge with Bridgeport or to pay the university rent for use of its campus. These efforts did not succeed. Merger was particularly unattractive because institutions were unwilling to take on Bridgeport's $22 million debt. The president of the university, Dr. Janet D. Greenwood, who had been appointed to succeed Lee Miles in August 1987, resigned in November 1991, less than a month after trustees rejected an offer from a group financed by the Unification Church to invest $50 million in the university. Faced with the alternatives of shutting down or reconsidering the World Peace Academy's offer, the trustees were advised by their lawyers that they had an obligation under the university's charter to enter into serious negotiations. With few alternatives, the Board accepted this offer in 1992. Disputes have continued, however.

Sources: Conversation between Alan Pifer and William G. Bowen, May 20, 1993; George Judson, "Slow Death on Campus," *New York Times,* December 2, 1991, B1; Laurie Goodstein, "Church Bids for Legitimacy; Moon's Group Wooed a City to Buy University," *Washington Post,* May 26, 1992, A1.

Notes

Preface

1. Sir Adrian Cadbury, "Reflections on Corporate Governance," Ernest Sykes Memorial Lecture, March 11, 1993, London, 1.

2. *New York Times,* August 21, 1993, Editorial, 18.

3. See Leslie Wayne, "Exporting Shareholder Activism," *New York Times,* July 16, 1993, D1.

4. Two relatively recent booklength studies of the for-profit sector, each containing many references to earlier work, are: Jay W. Lorsch, *Pawns or Potentates: The Reality of America's Corporate Boards,* Boston, MA: Harvard Business School Press, 1989, and Charles N. Waldo, *Boards of Directors: Their Changing Roles, Structure, and Information Needs,* Westport, CT: Quorum Books, 1985. For an historical account, see John L. Weinberg, "Status and Functions of Corporate Directors," Undergraduate Thesis, Princeton University, April 1948. Much of the current literature on corporate governance appears in journals and serial publications.

   Publications on the nonprofit sector include, among many others: Brian O'Connell, *The Board Member's Book,* New York: Foundation Center, 1985; Cyril O. Houle, *Governing Boards,* San Francisco: Jossey-Bass, 1989; and a most useful series of pamphlets also published by the National Center for Nonprofit Boards as its "Governance Booklets." Some studies also focus on individual fields.

For example, there is a comprehensive study of boards of trustees at independent liberal arts and comprehensive colleges (Richard P. Chait, Thomas P. Holland, and Barbara E. Taylor, *The Effective Board of Trustees,* Phoenix, AZ: Oryx Press, 1993).

Chapter 1

1. See Appendix B for capsule summaries of these cases (as well as others), including references to press accounts.

2. Among the many accounts of this controversy, see, for example, Johnnie L. Roberts and Randall Smith, "The Plot Thickens: Who Gets the Blame for Paramount Gaffes?" *The Wall Street Journal,* Dec. 13, 1993, A1.

3. This was accomplished through the National Museum of the American Indian Act, Public Law 101–185, November 28, 1989. See Appendix B for references and additional details.

4. See, for example, the range of views expressed, and the studies cited, in the *Report of the Subcouncil on Corporate Governance and Financial Markets to the Competitiveness Policy Council,* March 1993, including both "Concurring Views and Rejoinder" by John Pound and "Dissenting and Concurring Views" by Martin Lipton and Jay W. Lorsch.

5. See William T. Allen, "Redefining the Role of Outside Directors in an Age of Global Competition," address at the Ray Garrett, Jr., Corporate and Securities Law Institute, Northwestern University, April 30, 1992, 7. Sir Adrian Cadbury discusses "governance by takeover" in "Reflections on Corporate Governance" (Ernest Sykes Memorial Lecture, March 11, 1993, 7).

6. See, for example, John Pound, "Beyond Takeovers: Politics Comes to Corporate Control," *Harvard Business Review,* March/April 1992, 83–93.

7. "A Modest Proposal for Improved Corporate Governance," *Business Lawyer,* 98, (November 1992), 59–77.

8. *New York Times,* June 22, 1993, D1.

9. Bernard Black, "The Value of Institutional Investor Management: The Empirical Evidence," *UCLA Law Review,* 39 (1992): 501–554. This

article, originally prepared for the Competitiveness Council, contains extensive references to the journal literature.

10. The reference to scholarship, and keeping it "in its place," is from a famous essay by the economist Jacob Viner ("A Modest Proposal for More Emphasis on Scholarship in Graduate Training," in *The Long View and the Short,* Glencoe, IL: The Free Press, 1958). Viner was a passionate advocate of scholarship, and his essay is a classic exposition of the value of not overstating the case when arguing in favor of something that one really cares about.

11. See Virginia Hodgkinson et al., *Nonprofit Almanac, 1992–93: Dimensions of the Independent Sector,* San Francisco: Jossey-Bass, 1992 especially Chapter 1, and Lester M. Salamon, *America's Nonprofit Sector: A Primer,* New York: Foundation Center, 1992, Chapter 2. Several of us at the Mellon Foundation have just completed a booklength study describing and analyzing various "macro-level" dimensions of the nonprofit sector, including rates of growth in the number of entities with tax-exempt rulings in various fields, their geographical distribution, and trends in their sizes and revenue profiles. This study by William G. Bowen, Thomas I. Nygren, Sarah E. Turner, and Elizabeth A. Duffy is tentatively titled "The Charitable Nonprofits: An Institutional Analysis" and is scheduled to be published by Jossey-Bass in the fall of 1994.

12. Sarah E. Turner and William G. Bowen, "The Flight from the Arts and Sciences: Trends in Degrees Conferred," *Science,* October 26, 1990, especially 517–518.

13. For a detailed description of governmental oversight responsibilities in the state of New York, see Allen R. Bromberger and Catherine L. Woodman, (Eds.), *Advising Nonprofits,* New York: Council of New York Law Associates, 3rd ed., 1990. The potential power of the attorney general (AG), exercised through the Charities Bureau, is great. The AG is a necessary party in all proceedings involving charitable dispositions and must approve petitions to incorporate, to amend a certificate of incorporation, to merge or consolidate, to sell all or substantially all of a corporation's assets, or dissolve. The AG has the right to sue to enforce rights given to members, officers, and directors; and the AG can also sue to remove directors and officers, to dissolve a corporation, and to appoint a receiver.

See Daniel L. Kurtz, *Board Liability: Guide for Nonprofit Directors,* Mount Kisco, NY: Moyer Bell Ltd., 1988, for a further discussion of both liabilities and the legal oversight of the nonprofit sector in New York. Kurtz describes the government's relative lack of interest in policing nonprofits, and notes (p. 93): "In 1985, for example, only 13 states reported a total of 33 law suits brought by attorneys general involving charities at all, and a number of those dealt with professional fund-raisers, fraudulent charities, and with legislative and other initiatives entirely outside the law enforcement area. Only a handful of matters reported raised any questions concerning the conduct of officers and directors."

14. See Daniel L. Kurtz, "Standing," unpublished paper presented before the Nonprofit Forum, December 1992, and Mary Grace Blasko, Curt S. Crossley, and David Lloyd, "Standing to Sue in the Charitable Sector," unpublished paper, New York: New York University, 1993. In the for-profit case, any shareholder has the right to sue. Here the contrast between the sectors is especially sharp.

15. A lengthy excerpt from this letter of resignation was published in the *New York Times,* January 11, 1977, Section 1, 1.

Chapter 2

1. "Governance Is Governance," Occasional Paper, Washington, DC: Independent Sector, September 1987. This speech was given originally on May 7, 1985, and has (deservedly) attracted much attention. Here is what Dayton said at the time (p. 2): "Governance is governance. That's more than the title of a speech—it's a deeply held conviction. It's a conviction first of all that governance is not management, and second that governance in the independent sector . . . is absolutely identical to governance in the for-profit sector—with one added dimension [the 'volunteering' function of the director of a nonprofit corporation]."

2. William Shanklin, "Fortune 500 Dropouts," *Planning Review,* May 1986, 13.

3. See Daniel L. Kurtz, *Board Liability: Guide for Nonprofit Directors,* Mt. Kisco, NY: Moyer Bell Ltd., 1988, especially Chapters 1 and 4. See also Harvard Law Review Association, "Developments in the

Law: Nonprofit Corporations," 105:1578, 1992, especially 1592–1598.

4. Kurtz, 1988, 4. Also, a nonprofit considering a major change in its mission is required to notify the IRS. Notification is all that is required as long as charitable purposes are still being served.

5. Linda Snyder Hays, "Twenty-Five Years of Change in the Fortune 500," *Fortune,* May 5, 1980, 88–96.

6. For a discussion of the wide range of activities undertaken by the Bedford-Stuyvesant Restoration Corporation (into the fields of cultural enrichment, education, health, social services, and housing), see Patrice Miles, "Restoration: A Model CDC," *Black Enterprise, 23* (October 1992) 24.

7. This is the formulation of W. Taylor Reveley III, a Richmond lawyer with wide experience on nonprofit boards.

8. See "Beginning the Next Hundred Years," [The New York Public Library's Strategic Plan], April 8, 1992.

9. "Redefining the Role of Outside Directors in an Age of Global Competition," Luncheon Address, Ray Garret, Jr., Corporate and Securities Law Institute, Northwestern University, April 30, 1992, mimeo, 15.

10. Marion J. Levy, Jr., *Eleven Laws of the Disillusionment of the True Liberal,* Princeton, NJ: M. J. Levy, 1981, Law 10.

11. "Governance Is Governance," 1987, 3.

Chapter 3

1. Council on Foundations, *Foundation Management Report,* 7th ed., 1993, 2.

2. W. Taylor Reveley, "The Problem of the Feckless Board," Memorandum dated August 24, 1992, 3.

3. *The Wall Street Journal,* December 9, 1993, A1.

4. Korn/Ferry International, *Board of Directors Nineteenth Annual Study,* 1992, 4. The SpencerStuart Board Index (SSBI) shows the average size of a board in its universe as having declined to 13 from 15 five years ago (*SpencerStuart Board Index: 1993 Proxy Report,* 3).

5. American Symphony Orchestra League, *Policies and Procedures of Orchestra Governing Boards,* Washington, D.C.: American Symphony Orchestra League, 1991, 4–5.

6. Korn/Ferry, *Nineteenth Annual Board of Directors Study,* 1992, 7, and Table 1. See also the *SpencerStuart Board Index: 1993 Proxy Report,* 3, for similar data.

7. *SpencerStuart Board Index: 1993 Proxy Report,* 3.

8. Irving Janis, *Groupthink: Psychological Studies of Policy Decisions and Fiascoes,* rev. ed., Boston, MA: Houghton Mifflin, 1983, especially 9, 13. This book is an analysis of the Bay of Pigs invasion and other examples of serious miscalculations in the foreign policy arena.

9. Donald S. Perkins, "20 Questions of Corporate Governance," 1992 CEO Forum on Corporate Governance, Wharton School of Finance and Commerce, University of Pennsylvania, September 9, 1992, mimeo, 9. Perkins is objecting to efforts to "assure independence" through "corporate governance definitions and perhaps legislation."

10. The Council of Institutional Investors, a Washington, D.C.-based group of pension funds, has a policy against all such links. Anne S. Hansen, deputy director of the Council, is quoted as saying: "What that means is that the person has never worked at the company, is not related to someone who has worked at that company, and does not provide services to that company like a lawyer or vendor might." (Alison Cowan, "Boards Protect Shareholders, Right?" *New York Times,* July 11, 1993, Section 3, 8.)

11. In *Corporate Culture and Performance,* New York: Free Press, 1992, Kotter and Haskett assemble considerable empirical evidence to reject the commonly held view that "strong cultures create excellent performance." Numerous company histories are discussed, including that of GM.

12. "Governance Is Governance," Occasional Paper, Washington, D.C.: Independent Sector, September 1987 (based on talk given May 7, 1985), 5–6.

13. Korn/Ferry, *Board of Directors Nineteenth Annual Survey,* 1992, 14.

14. For a strong statement of this position, see William A. Sahlman, "Why Sane People Shouldn't Serve on Public Boards," *Harvard Business Review,* May–June 1990, no. 3, 28.

15. The reference to "volunteers" is from an account of the Empire Blue Cross-Blue Shield debacle. Salvatore R. Curiale, the New York state insurance superintendent, harshly criticized the board of Empire for having "sat on its hands." In response, Harold E. Vogt explained: "Everyone of the Board members is a *volunteer* [emphasis added]," *New York Times,* April 17, 1993, 16. Section 1, 23.

16. *New York Times,* August 21, 1993, Editorial, Section 1, 18.

17. Memorandum to William G. Bowen from Jeffrey Brinck, Esq., Milbank, Tweed, Hadley & McCloy. Another attorney, Daniel Kurtz, concurs: "Courts tend not to impose harsh penalties on volunteer directors for their actions or inaction" (Daniel Kurtz, *Board Liability: Guide for Nonprofit Directors,* Mount Kisco, NY: Moyer Bell Limited, 1988, 94.)

18. Jane Fritsch, "At Empire, the Glow of Greed," *New York Times,* July 11, 1993, Section 4, 20.

Chapter 4

1. Graef Crystal, *In Search of Excess,* New York: W.W. Norton, 1991.

2. One person associated prominently with this idea for some years is Ira Millstein, who has spoken frequently on this subject and who wrote an article in 1988 with Winthrop Knowlton suggesting the advantages of this model ("Can the Board of Directors Help the American Corporation Earn the Immortality It Holds So Dear?" in John R. Meyer and James M. Gustafson, (eds.), *The U.S. Business Corporation: An Institution in Transition,* Cambridge, MA: Ballinger Pub. Co., 1988, Chapter 9). See also Jay W. Lorsch with Elizabeth MacIver, *Pawns or Potentates: The Reality of America's Corporate Boards,* Boston, MA: Harvard Business School Press, 1989, and the more recent article by Martin Lipton and Jay Lorsch, "A Modest Proposal for Improved Corporate Governance," *Business Lawyer,* November 1992, 59–77. Most recently, Leslie Levy has written a special report on this topic ("Separate Chairmen of the Board: Their Rules, Legal Liabilities, and Compensation," Institute for Research on Boards of Directors, Sarasota, FL, 1993). Both Lorsch and Levy discuss the history of this concept. In Britain, this subject is treated in the widely discussed *Report of the Cadbury Committee on the Financial Aspects of Corporate Governance,* London: GEE, 1992.

3. Speech given on May 7, 1985, and reprinted under the title "Governance Is Governance," Washington, D.C.: Independent Sector, 1987, 7–8.

4. Lorsch, 1988, 91ff, especially 93, 96.

5. The 1992 Korn/Ferry survey reports: "74 percent of all CEOs surveyed (and 85 percent of those at $5 billion-plus companies) see no advantage to separating the chairman and chief executive officer functions, up from 68 percent last year" (7).

6. See Levy, "Separate Chairmen," 1993, 3–4, He has surveyed the field carefully and also fails to find examples of the long-term use of the separate chairman model.

7. "Dissenting and Concurring Views," in *The Will to Act: Report of the Subcouncil on Corporate Governance and Financial Markets to the Competitiveness Policy Council*, Washington, D.C.: Competitiveness Policy Council, March 1993, 158.

8. Dayton, 1988, 2.

9. "A Modest Proposal for Improved Corporate Governance," *Business Lawyer*, November 1992, 70–71.

10. See Michael W. Miller, "IBM, Overhauling Its Board, Will Create 'Governance' Panel of Outside Directors," *The Wall Street Journal*, July 30, 1993, A3. This new IBM committee will also handle issues of corporate public responsibility.

11. See Elisabeth Clarkson's response to the Beaman report in "Wilson College, A Case Study" (report prepared for discussion at the Lilly Endowment, October 10, 1979, by Alice L. Beeman, with comments by Elisabeth Hudnut Clarkson).

12. *Nineteenth Annual Board of Directors Study*, 1992, 1.

13. See the Lipton and Lorsch paper, "A Modest Proposal for Improved Corporate Governance," *Business Lawyer*, November 1992, 69–70; the Dayton-Hudson wheel is reproduced as exhibit 1.

14. See Johnnie L. Roberts and Randall Smith, "The Plot Thickens: Who Gets the Blame for Paramount Gaffes?" *The Wall Street Journal*, Dec. 13, 1993, A1; and Barry Layne, "One-Day Sale! Par Board Sets Monday for Bids," *Hollywood Reporter*, December 15, 1993, 1.

15. See Beaman and Clarkson, "Wilson College, A Case Study." The Wilson College case is also discussed in the more general study, *Colleges and Corporate Change: Merger, Bankruptcy, and Closure,* by Joseph O'Neill and Samuel Barnett, Princeton, NJ: Conference-University Press, 1980.

16. Madeleine F. Green, *The American College President: A Contemporary Profile,* American Council on Education, 1988, 18; Courtney Leatherman, "Typical President Is White, Male, 54 Years Old," *Chronicle of Higher Education,* September 15, 1993, A19.

17. The classic reference is Adolph A. Berle and Gardiner C. Means, *The Modern Corporation and Private Property,* New York: Macmillan, 1932. As John Weinberg noted in his thesis (p. 3), Adam Smith had called attention to the same phenomena in *The Wealth of Nations,* (1776): "The directors of such companies . . . being managers rather of other people's money than their own, it cannot well be expected that they should watch over [it] with the same anxious vigilance with which the partnership in a private co-partner frequently watch over their own. . . . Negligence and profusion, therefore, must always prevail more or less." The subsequent rise of the pension fund is discussed in Peter F. Drucker, *The Unseen Revolution: How Pension Fund Socialism Came to America,* New York: Harper & Row, 1976.

18. *The American College and University: A History,* New York: Alfred A. Knopf, 1962, especially Chapter 19, 408, 427.

19. "Redefining the Role of Outside Directors in an Age of Global Competition," address at Northwestern University, April 30, 1992, mimeo, 8.

Chapter 5

1. A recent book by James McGee and Laurence Prusak (*Managing Information Strategically,* New York: John Wiley & Sons, 1993) provides both a systematic discussion of the subject from a business point of view and a useful bibliographic essay (225–238).

2. See the reference to the interest in this question by Ralph Cordiner, then CEO of General Electric, back in 1951, in Robert G. Eccles and Nitin Nohria, *Beyond the Hype: Rediscovering the*

Essence of Management, Boston, MA: Harvard Business School Press, 1992, as cited in Lipton and Lorsch, "A Modest Proposal," 1992, 71.

3. Specific reference is made to projects being carried out by the American Institute of Certified Public Accountants and the Financial Executives Institute (see pp. 142–143 of *The Will To Act,* Washington DC: Competitiveness Policy Council, March 1993). Mention should also be made of an earlier study by Charles N. Waldo, *Boards of Directors: Their Changing Roles, Structure, and Information Needs,* Westport, CT: Quorum Books, 1985. A major thrust of this book is "the critical need for relevant information," and the last half is devoted to this subject.

4. See "Court Ruling Boosts QVC in Paramount Takeover Bid," *Chicago Tribune,* November 25, 1993, Business section, 1; see also *The Wall Street Journal,* December 13, 1993, A1.

5. Available from The Andrew W. Mellon Foundation, 140 E. 62nd Street, New York, NY, 10021. The citations for the exposure drafts are FASB, *Proposed Statement of Financial Accounting Standards, Accounting for Contributions Received and Contributions Made and Capitalization of Works of Art, Historical Treasures, and Similar Assets,* Exposure Draft, Norwalk, CT, October 31, 1990; and *Proposed Statement of Financial Accounting Standards, Financial Statements of Not-for-Profit Organizations,* Exposure Draft, Norwalk, CT, October 23, 1992. In June 1993, FASB released two publications stating its conclusions: *Statement of Financial Accounting Standards No. 116, Accounting for Contributions Received and Contributions Made,* and *Financial Accounting Standards No. 117, Financial Statements of Not-for-Profit Organizations.* See Robert H. Mallott, "In Search of the Bottom Line," *Trusteeship,* January/February 1994, 14–20 for an account of one Trustee's effort to reform the reporting system at the University of Chicago along similar lines.

6. See "Warehouses of Wealth: The Tax-Free Economy," *Philadelphia Inquirer,* April 18, 1993, through April 24, 1993. The quotation in the text is from the April 18, 1993, issue, 15.

7. Gordon C. Winston, "The Capital Costs Conundrum," *NACUBO Business Officer,* June 1993: "At Williams College the cost of

producing a year of education for a student in 1991 appears to be $33,600. When one conservatively accounts for the use of capital, the cost rises to $51,000" (p. 22). Arjay Miller has pointed out that the use of historical costs to value assets in for-profit industries such as railroads and autos can create somewhat analogous problems, especially if the assets were obtained a long time ago.

8. See Seth Mydans, "Where Trouble Is Rare and Governing Is Easy," *New York Times,* September 10, 1993, A18.

9. L. V. Jones, G. Lindzey, and P. W. Coggeshall, (Eds.), *An Assessment of Research-Doctorate Programs in the United States,* 5 vols., Washington, D.C.: National Academy Press, 1982.

10. *Data Report from the 1989 National Museum Survey,* January 1992.

Chapter 6

1. Chronicle of Higher Education, March 10, 1993.

2. See Henry Hansmann's article on endowments ("Why Do Universities Have Endowments?" *Journal of Legal Studies,* 19 [1990], 3–42) for a detailed discussion that focuses specifically on intergenerational issues. A recent article in *Museum News* (Stephen E. Weill, "The Deaccession Cookie Jar," November/December 1992) illustrates well the difficulty of making current versus future trade-offs when confronted with pressures to sell art works in order to address budgetary problems.

3. Marion J. Levy, Jr., *Eleven Laws of the Disillusionment of the True Liberal,* Princeton, NJ: M. J. Levy, 1981, Law 1.

Index